Shorter Walks Near Hungerford

by Alex Milne-White

MW
BOOKS LIMITED
Published by Milne-White Books Limited

First Edition

Published by Milne-White Books Ltd.

ISBN 978–09570027–2–2

Copyright © 2016 Milne-White Books Ltd

All photography by Alex Milne-White
www.hungerfordbooks.co.uk

Typesetting and illustration by www.thewordservice.com

Printed by The Mayfield Press, Oxford

Shorter Walks Near Hungerford

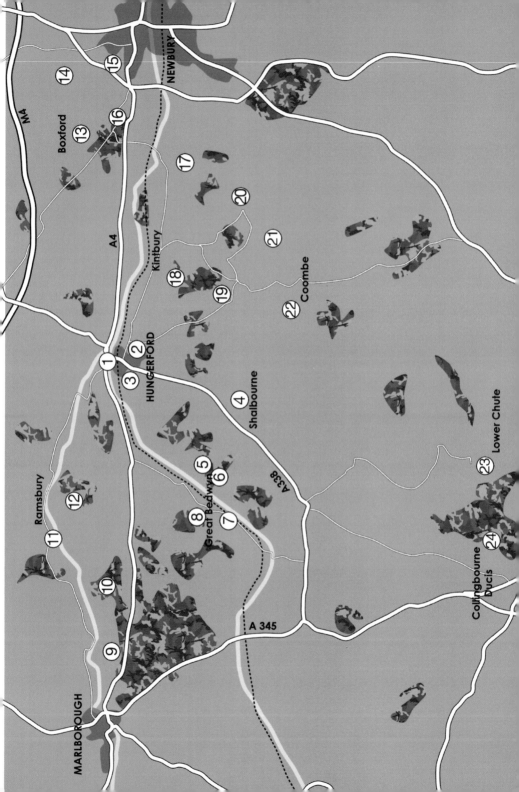

Contents

Introduction

In the introduction to my previous book *Pub Walks Near Hungerford* I waxed lyrical about the Red Kites that were starting to appear in the skies over West Berkshire, If you were lucky you might catch a glimpse of one or two circling majestically over a neighbouring field. Now, six years later, they're everywhere, on any walk or even driving down the A4 you'll see loads of the things (often in a squashed mess on the road), they're a bit like rural pigeons. Having said all that I still love to see them gliding through the skies so I'm not complaining really.

The first book was aimed at people who liked a fair walk (most were 5 or 6 miles in length), but were not averse to stopping for a drink and/or some grub along the way (hence the pubs). For many though 5 or 6 miles is a bit of a stretch, and for others the idea of trying to drag their children (who have boundless energy when it suits them, but can apparently become tired after 100 meters when it doesn't) that far causes palpitations. So this is the book for them, and for anyone who just fancies a less strenuous walk when the weather's fair.

All the walks are circular and between 2 and 5 miles in length, with most between 3 and 4 miles long. I would have liked to have made them all pub walks again, but it quickly became apparent that this was unrealistic with shorter walks. The walks are all original (as far as I'm aware) although some shared sections with walks in the first book are inevitable and I've tried to identify walks that would be suitable for families, dog walkers and even families with a baby/toddler in a pram/stroller (although this proved pretty difficult to find).

So I've given each walk a hill and nettle rating (out of 3), plus in the introductory blurb for each one I've tried to suggest how dog or pram friendly the walk might be, based on the number/type of stiles there are and quality of the paths. Most of the walks were tested in August/September so I've also noted where there might be rich blackberry pickings to be had, this, and the nettle rating, will be pretty irrelevant if you walking in Spring, but if you have a child, like I do, who seems to be magnetically attracted to even the tiniest nettle, then you might find it quite useful.

Judging dog friendliness was a bit tricky for me as I've never walked a dog in my life, and all dogs are different anyway, but hopefully the comments will be useful for some. Walks with few or no stiles can often make good running routes too if the grounds not too muddy.

I originally tried to start the research for this book in 2013, with a 5-month-old Oscar strapped to my chest, but I'd only got about half a mile before it became apparent that this wasn't even close to his idea of a fun outing and I had to turn back and wait another 2 years until I had enough time to do it all on my own.

Unlike the previous book the given walk distances should be accurate as I used a GPS watch to measure them, although adjustments did have to be made when I accidentally went off course (which happened quite often, especially in Wiltshire, where footpath signs seem to be an optional extra). The walk times though are obviously estimates based on how long it took me, they will take much longer if you're dragging children along for instance.

All walks are covered by Ordnance Survey Explorer maps 157 & 158, apart from the final 2 which are on Explorer 131. Although I'd like to think that all the instructions are as thorough and foolproof as possible, if you do find you have strayed from the path the relevant map is pretty useful for finding your way back again.

Key to maps:

These symbols indicate properties of the walks:

◉ OS Map equivalent

✐ Distance of walk

◷ Estimated duration of walk

⊗ Not suitable for dogs

⊗ Not suitable for prams

🍇 Good chance of berries in season

These symbols are a rating from 1–3:

▲▲ Hills

🌿 Nettles

These symbols represent buildings:

 Church

 Grand House

Pub

 Farm

1. Hungerford to Leverton

Just 1 stile so pretty dog friendly, stile and steps mean pram friendly only with 2 adults.

This walk starts in the centre of Hungerford and heads up to the big oak on the hill that you can see from pretty much anywhere in Hungerford, and which in turn gives you a great view of the area when you get up there. You then head across to Leverton with its lovely row of thatched cottages. Leverton is a remarkably complete survival of an 18th/19th century estate village, belonging to the Chilton Lodge estate. The stocks are a replica of the originals, which were taken to the Ashmolean Museum in the 1990s. You then head back to Hungerford via Eddington.

Park anywhere on **Hungerford High Street** or in the **Church Street car park** (next to the library).

1. Walk towards the canal bridge, then past the **Tutti Pole** Café down to the canal towpath and turn left. Proceed on **Kennet & Avon** towpath past the first lock, then cross the swing bridge next to **St Lawrence's Church**.
2. Go through gate, following **yellow footpath arrow**, then same again with next gate and over a metal and concrete bridge over the **River Dunn**. Go through another gate, following **yellow footpath arrow** and left along obvious path.
3. When you reach a **footpath junction sign** (missing some of its arrows currently) go right, through a gate with another **yellow footpath arrow**, then immediately left at next footpath junction.
4. Go diagonally across field on clear path, through another gate and up to the **A4**, bear slightly left then cross carefully over road to **footpath sign** pointing up some steps, follow this path up and over stile.
5. Follow path along left edge of field, with great views of **Hungerford** behind you, and when you reach large tree with bench dogleg slightly left to follow right edge of neighbouring field.
6. Aim for gap at bottom right corner of field then follow public footpath sign through copse and straight on across field and down to main road. Cross road carefully and turn right along pavement and walk for about **300 meters** (crossing back into Berkshire) until you see a **footpath sign** pointing left through small gap in hedge.
7. Go down steps and across bridge over the **River Kennet**, then another bridge, then right on obvious path. Stay on path, following **yellow arrow** to cross another bridge and along track towards large gate.
8. Go through gate and along passing **Leverton Cottages** on your right, then turn right on road for about **500 meters** to a road junction. Turn right, signposted for **Eddington** and **Hungerford**, and immediately you will see a footpath just to the right of the road.
9. Follow this path to its end then go straight on following **public footpath sign** down gravel drive then left on path to an orchard. Go straight on then right, heading for the right corner of the orchard.
10. Follow **public footpath sign** down narrow path between 2 houses and over bridge, then go left on clear path all the way to the end of **Oxford Street**. Turn right and right again on main road over bridge, then bear left at mini-roundabout.
11. Cross at Zebra crossing and continue to next mini-roundabout, turn left up **Bridge Street**, crossing road at the zebra crossing, then over canal bridge and back to your starting point.

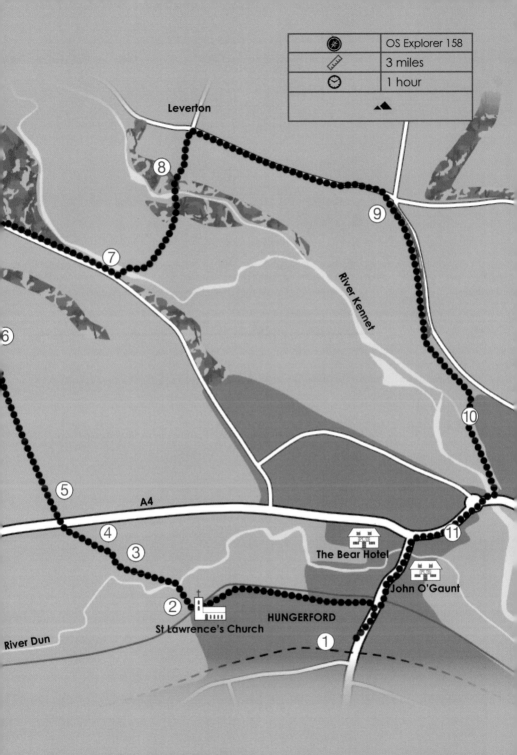

Leverton

⑧

⑨

River Kennet

⑦

⑥

⑩

⑤

A4

④

③

The Bear Hotel

⑪

② St Lawrence's Church

John O'Gaunt

HUNGERFORD

River Dun

①

11

2. Hungerford Common and Marsh

This walk was patched together from a couple of walks that I devised for Hungerford Town Council to use for a leaflet of short local walks showcasing the local area. (They then produced the leaflets without acknowledgement or thanks, but never mind.)

The walk passes most of the shops and pubs in Hungerford (purely by coincidence), 2 sections of the canal and both of the local public green spaces; Hungerford common and Freeman's Marsh. Freeman's Marsh is home to many wild birds, plants and animals - some of which are now rare in southern England. More than 100 species have been identified of both resident and migrating birds. These numbers are quite extraordinary for a limited area of countryside.

Park anywhere you can in the centre of Hungerford.

1. Walk up the **High Street** past **The Hungerford Bookshop**, the **Hungerford Arms** pub and various antiques shops for about 5 minutes, then cross road at **The Borough Arms** pub and walk to the left of white railings.

2. Go through gap between houses and up the alley. Cross the road at the top onto **South View** and follow this road, past the **Hungerford Primary School**, as the road turns into a footpath leading to **Hungerford Common**.

3. Follow path straight on for about 20m then turn left to pass the car park of **The Downgate** pub.

4. Cross the road then follow a faint path to the right until a path crosses to the left, follow this and look out for a clump of trees behind which is a tunnel under the railway.

5. Go through the tunnel and then turn left before the fence and follow the grassy path to a gate at the end, go through gate and turn left on towpath then cross the **Kennet and Avon Canal** at the bridge and follow the footpath to emerge onto **Bridge Street** next to the **John O'Gaunt** pub.

6. Turn right past **Furr & Co** then turn left at **The Bear Hotel**. Walk down the A4 for about 5 minutes, past **The Sun Inn**, until you see a Footpath sign on the left.

7. Follow the path down a track then a path to the left at the end of the track. At junction of footpaths turn left over stream, and then right at next footpath junction.

8. Go through gate into **Freeman's Marsh**, then along and over a small bridge. Follow stream on your right until you see a **footpath sign** pointing diagonally left, follow this in direction of **Swing Bridge**, crossing a small concrete bridge on the way.

9. Cross swing bridge and turn left. Go through gate onto canal towpath and follow all the way to **St Lawrence church**. Go half right through church yard then left on road, past **Hungerford Nursery School**, down alley way and back onto the **High Street**.

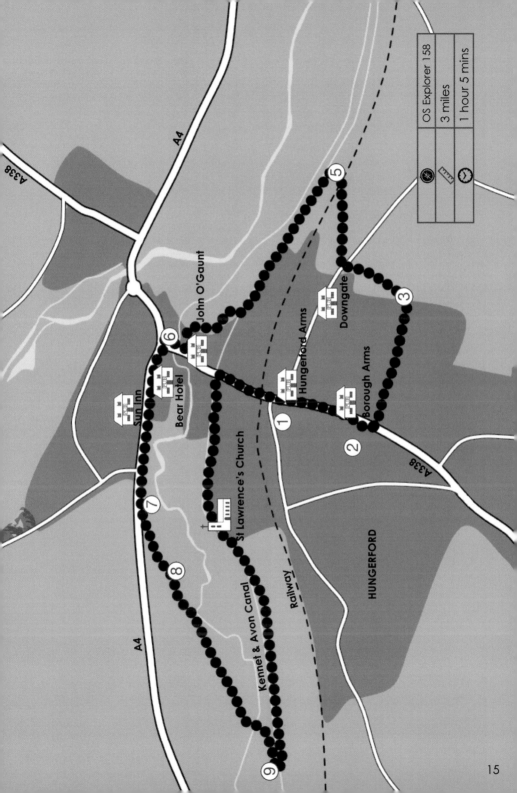

OS Explorer 158

3 miles

1 hour 5 mins

A4

A338

A4

A338

John O'Gaunt

Sun Inn

Bear Hotel

St Lawrence's Church

Kennet & Avon Canal

Railway

Hungerford Arms

Downgate

Borough Arms

HUNGERFORD

1

2

3

5

6

7

8

9

15

3. West Hungerford and Standen Manor

There is one small section with 2 stiles and 2 lots of steps, but this could be avoided by going right on the road, at the end of step 7, back to the start.

As with most walks, if you live near the starting point you'll probably know the walk already, and we used to live very close to this one. It's the longest walk in this book, at 5 miles, and would have made it into the last book were it not for the absence of any pubs along the way. Surprisingly for of walk of this length it's mostly flat and stile free until quite near the end when you have to cross a 2 stiles and go up and down some steps to cross the railway line, but as mentioned above you could divert onto the little used road for the last section to avoid this bit.

Standen Manor (in earlier days also known as South Standen or Standen Hussey) is an extremely attractive, Grade II Listed country mansion. Pevsner describes it as early 18th century, with blue headers and red dressings. Six bay front, with parapet, hipped roof, segment headed windows, widely spread.

The walk starts from **Smitham Bridge Road**, at the beginning of **Marsh Lane**, next to the playground. From **Hungerford High Street** drive down **Church Road**, past the **Library** (if it's still there) and **Fire station** and keep going until you see the playground on your right, park somewhere here.

1. Opposite the end of **Marsh Lane** there is a **public footpath sign**, follow this clear path across the field towards gap in trees. Go through gap and continue in same direction towards end of copse (or you can skirt left edge of field if easier).

2. At edge of copse bear slightly left, following **footpath sign**, along left edge of field, then at end of field go straight on along smaller path winding right to a gate with a **yellow footpath arrow**.

3. Go through gate and follow clear path through trees to a large kissing gate, then along, past **yellow footpath arrow** on tree, to the corner of a field. Go left and follow left edge of this field.

4. When the field bears right you will see a gate on the left with **footpath arrow**, go through and follow direction of arrow across field, aiming left of all the buildings of **Standen Manor** you can see, then when you can see some gates aim for those.

5. Go through large kissing gate next to large metal one then turn right on lane and follow this past buildings on either side. When the lane bears left you will see a **bridleway sign** pointing left and a **footpath sign** pointing straight on, go straight on.

6. Bear left of farm buildings on track, following another **footpath sign**, then go through large metal gate and carry straight on along path between two fields. Keep following this path in the direction of the telegraph poles until at the corner of the field you will see a **footpath sign** and **footpath arrow**.

7. Take this clear path on clearing through woods then follow another **yellow footpath arrow** onto path between wooden fences. Stay on this path, which is quite muddy in places, until you reach a small road, then cross and follow **public footpath sign** opposite.

8. At the end of short path turn right, following **public footpath sign** onto wide tree-lined track. At the end of track turn right, following **yellow footpath arrow**, then when this path opens onto field follow **footpath arrow** along left edge of field.

9. Go over stile on the right, then turn right to go up steps to the railway track, cross carefully and descend steps down to another stile then turn right. You can go along left edge of field or on fairly clear path straight across towards gap in trees.

10. You can veer left at any point to the canal towpath, but the path goes through the gap in trees and straight on to a gate at far end of field. Go through gate onto **Marsh Lane** and continue to the end of the lane and your starting point.

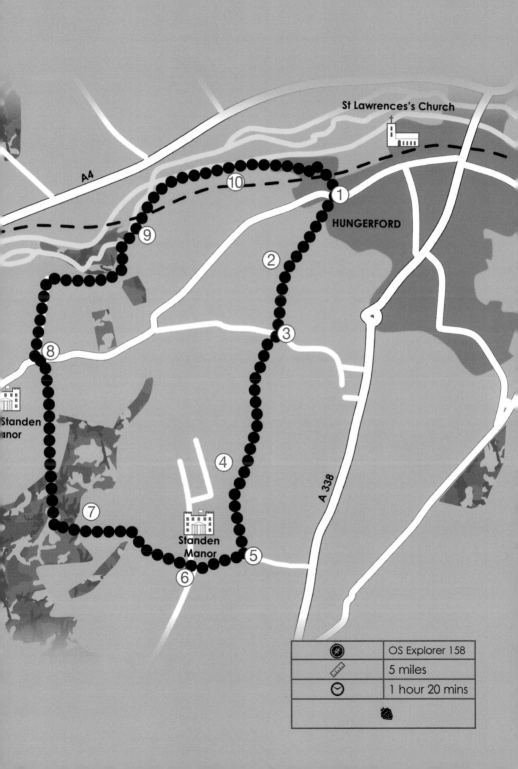

4. Shalbourne Circuit

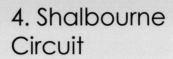

Dog friendly and just about pram friendly on main route, there is an alternative, slightly longer (2.6 miles) walk, but this does have stiles so wouldn't be pram friendly.

Shalbourne is a fairly large village that is apparently in some danger of losing its pub and shop/post office at the time of writing, hopefully this won't come to pass as Shalbourne should be comfortably big enough to support them. It's a lovely village especially when they all pull together for local events like the May Day fair and Classic Car Show.

There are lots of possible walks from Shalbourne, you can walk to Ham or Great Bedwyn (see *Pub Walks Near Hungerford*), but I've just chosen a shortish circuit around the west and north of the village for this book. I almost added a figure of 8 walk to Ham and back, but the route is so blindingly obvious I thought anyone local would know it already and anyone else could work it out from a quick glance at the OS map.

Park at **The Plough** or anywhere along the straight bit of road to the north of it.

1. Walk north along main road until you see a **Byway** sign pointing to the left, follow path down hill.

2. As you emerge from the shady byway there is a **footpath** crossing left to right, but carry straight on on **byway**, climbing up the hill.

3. At the top cross the road carefully and follow concrete track signed **Newtown Store.**

4. As you approach farm buildings take a right turn on track to where you can see a **footpath** sign.

5. Follow footpath around to the left, then right, then left again where the path forks. After **100 meters** there is a bridleway sign pointing right and you want to follow tree-lined path rather than the one along the edge of the field.

6. After about **200 meters** there is a **footpath** heading off to the right, ignore this one and you will soon come to a kind of crossroads of paths, head straight on and slightly right down a muddy looking path.

7. The path is a bit chopped up by hooves, but after **100 meters** a footpath forks off to the right, follow this until it rejoins a larger track.

8. You will immediately come to another track heading left to right and an inviting looking path straight ahead. Do not follow any of these paths; instead follow a completely unmarked path (as far as I could see) diagonally across the field to the left aiming for the left edge of the row of trees to the right.

9. Once you're about a 3rd of the way across the field you will see a house that you will skirt to its left and soon you will also see a small **footpath** sign confirming that you're not just tramping across a random field!

10. Take a right past the sign and down to the road, go left on the road for about 20 meters then cross carefully and follow footpath sign along right edge of field.

11. Keep the trees to your right to cross a footbridge at the corner of the field, then keep to right edge of next field until you reach a footpath heading off to left and right.

12. Take the footpath right, across field and down someone's drive to the main road.

13. Cross the road and head up the road opposite towards the church. Turn left just before the graveyard and follow this path until you emerge next to **Shalbourne Primary School.** Turn right on the road until you reach you starting point.

Alternative, slightly longer, route which has stiles.

14. Carry straight on to pass through a gap in corner of field, then cross the road and follow signed footpath round to the right.

15. Cross stile and carry straight on to another stile, cross this and head straight across   field, just right of some trees, to a kissing gate at far corner. Turn right onto **Cox's lane** and follow down to the main road and your starting point.

16. vv

22

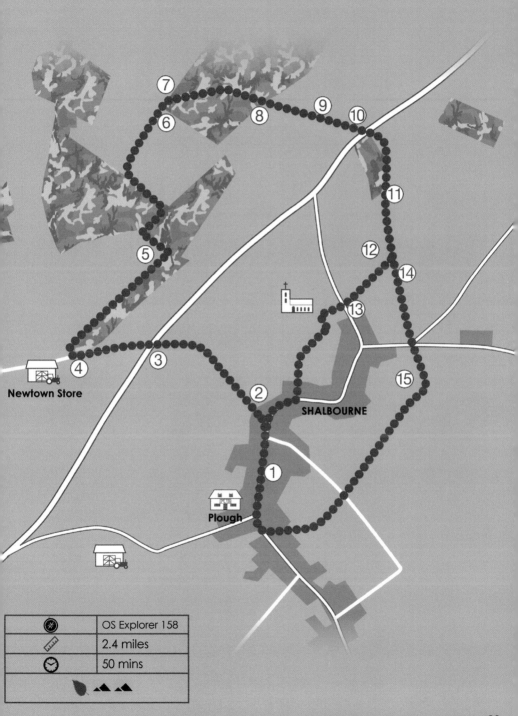

Newtown Store

SHALBOURNE

Plough

⊛	OS Explorer 158
📏	2.4 miles
⊘	50 mins

5. Little Bedwyn

Little Bedwyn is a picturesque
village situated on the Kennet
and Avon Canal and the railway
line between Hungerford and
Great Bedwyn. It has no pub
or shops, but instead has a
wonderful Michelin starred
restaurant called The Harrow.
It is also apparently home to
Gillian Anderson if Wikipedia is to
believed.

Towards the end of the walk you
pass through Sandy's Wood, next
to the church, which has trees
sponsored by local residents.
There is also a wildflower
meadow here.

As this walk is in Wiltshire there
are virtually no public footpath
signs so you'll just need to follow
the instructions carefully.

Park on NW side of railway near footbridge.

1. Walk over railway and canal footbridge and continue straight on road. Turn right at crossroads and when the road bears right, turn left and go through small gate, between paddocks and through another gate.
2. Turn left onto road, then right at T junction passing **The Harrow** restaurant, and after 100 meters there is a kissing gate on left, go through and go diagonally across field on fairly well trodden path.
3. Cross over 2 adjacent stiles at far end of field, then through gate into another field. On the **OS map** the path continues diagonally across field, but this is not possible, so skirt along right edge of field and when you reach a wooden fence bear left, with the fence to your right until you reach a stile on your right.
4. Cross stile and follow clear path across field to another stile, cross that and proceed to edge of field and across a high stile and down to the road.
5. Turn left on road, then when the road bears right turn left on unmarked track. Towards the end of the short track a bridleway crosses left and right, follow this to the right.
6. After **300 meters** there is an unmarked path to the left, ignore this and carry on for another **400 meters**, to another unmarked path on the left passing between wooden posts onto a tree-lined footpath.
7. The path becomes narrower and a bit nettley towards the end, and finishes onto a bridleway. Turn left then immediately fork right on wide footpath. As you round the corner up the hill a small, again unmarked, footpath peels off to the left, it doesn't look like it, but this is the correct path and soon opens into a broad tree lined path.
8. The path turns into a track as it passes a house then leads you to the road, cross the road* and go over the footbridge, between 2 houses to a metal gate. Go through and carefully cross the railway then another metal gate.
9. Turn left and, keeping the railway to your left, proceed until you reach a wooden gate. Go through and along the path through the small wood to a large gate. Skirt around the left of the churchyard until you reach a kissing gate. Go through and turn left on road back to your starting point.

*At this point you could turn left onto canal towpath and proceed until you reach the footbridge, then cross it back to your starting point.

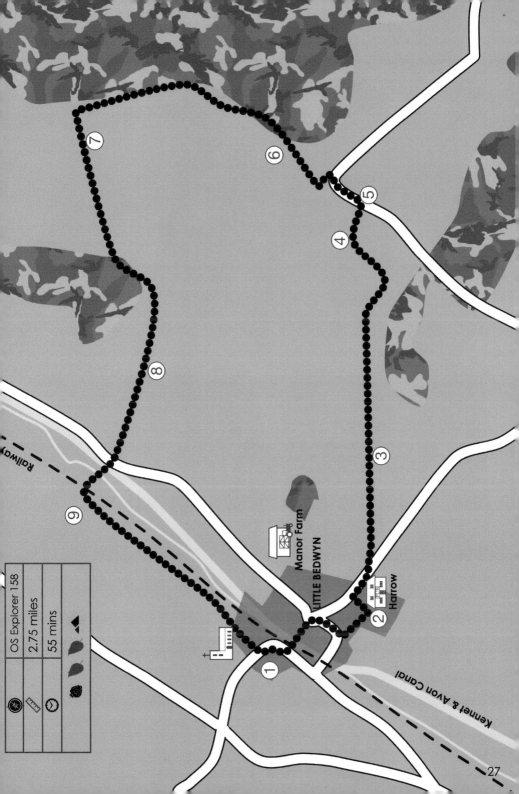

OS Explorer 158

2.75 miles

55 mins

Railway

Manor Farm

LITTLE BEDWYN

Harrow

Kennet & Avon Canal

6. Great Bedwyn and to the East

Dog friendly, but not really pram friendly as there are narrow and muddy paths along the way. Good for blackberries.

Great Bedwyn is the next (and usually last) train stop to the west of Hungerford and, like Little Bedwyn, is situated on the Kennet and Avon Canal. It is, according to its website, an idyllic English village with a vibrant community, numerous clubs, societies, as well as two village pubs, plus their own Post Office, Village Shop, Bakery and Hairdressers.

This walk is really a truncated version of the Great Bedwyn to Shalbourne circle in my previous book (*Pub Walks Near Hungerford*), but is a very nice walk in its own right so deserves a separate outing here.

There is a car park next to canal bridge, you can park there, or in **Great Bedwyn** and walk down to canal.

1. Go left (south-west) on canal towpath then as you reach a bridge over the canal turn left through gate take the path that goes straight up hill then curves right to proceed along right edge of field.
2. Go through gap in trees and along right edge of next field, and the same with the next gap, then into woods at far right corner of field onto slightly muddy path. As the woods open to a ferny clearing the path forks left and right, but you need to head for the big gap in the trees that is straight ahead.
3. Follow wide bumpy path between trees until it opens onto a field, the clear path carries straight on across field with another path forking back and right into the woods, ignore this path and carry on along edge of field to a path in the corner between 2 fences.
4. Narrow path opens into pleasant tree-lined path, then proceeds between 2 fields and down to the road. Turn left then cross road at T junction and follow **public bridleway** sign towards **Folly Farm** on track. Follow track round to the right.
5. Towards the end of the track there is a **footpath sign** to the left, follow this across field, past **waymark post**, then straight on aiming to skirt the left edge of woods, down the hill, then up again keeping the woods on your right until you see a track leading into woods.
6. Follow path past **yellow arrows** through trees, then after you emerge there is a **bridleway sign** pointing right and straight on, go straight on along edge of field and at end take the bridleway signposted left.
7. Follow long straight path gradually down hill, then round to the left until as it ends you see a sign marked '**Frogmore 1/2**' pointing right, follow that across grass, then gravel, then grass again onto path between trees.
8. Proceed gradually up the hill, then down again and look out on your left for a gap in the hedge where you will see **a public footpath sign** on a post. Go through gap and then diagonally across field towards another gap.
9. Go through and go straight on to skirt along right edge of houses. When you emerge onto track go left and follow down to the car park.

OS Explorer 158

3.33 miles

1 hour

Foxwood Farm

Folly Farm

7

6

5

4

8

3

9

Kennet & Avon C

GREAT BEDWYN

Cross Keys

1

2

Brail Farm

Three Tuns

Railway

31

7. Great Bedwyn and south west circuit

Not pram friendly due to a couple of stiles and some quite muddy stretches of path, should be fine for most dogs though.

You can visit St Mary's Church by taking a different route in step 8 of the walk and it is a Grade 1 listed building and contains the remains of several crusaders and a memorial to Sir John Seymour (1474-1536), father of King Henry VIII's wife, Jane Seymour.

The Bruce Trust operates several canal boats from the wharf in Great Bedwyn, providing disabled, disadvantaged or elderly people along with their family, friends or carer's, canal boat holidays and experience days.

Park somewhere along the High Street in **Bedwyn**.

1. Head up the road in the direction of the **Three Tuns** then take a left on **Back Lane**, next to the **Great Bedwyn Motor Co.** After about 200 meters you come to a crossroads, turn right on track, passing some allotments on your right.
2. Go through gate and continue in same direction on grassy path between 2 fields. At a junction of paths follow yellow footpath sign pointing left along muddy path up to a T-juntion where you turn right towards edge of trees.
3. At edge of wood footpath signs point forward left and back, go straight on along the edge of Shawgrove Copse, then cross stile and continue in same direction along left edge of field to another stile at far left corner.
4. Cross stile, following yellow footpath arrow in the same direction for about 20 meters then through a kissing gate on the left and into the woods. This short path leads to a drive, turn right on drive, then when you reach a junction of paths turn left.
5. Follow the wide, winding path through the woods, then when you come to a house on the left, go straight on along much narrower path. This muddy path joins with another muddy path, bear left on this.
6. The path becomes a rather nice tree-lined path as you emerge from the woods, carry straight on along Hatchet Lane until you reach a road junction, where you need to go straight on, signposted Wilton.
7. Go over railway and canal on road, then turn left on unmarked but clear path into field. This path doesn't appear on the OS map, but is clear and well-used and runs parallel to the canal along a long narrow field.
8. As the field narrows take the lower of two paths along to a gate on the left, go through gate and turn right on the Kennet & Avon canal towpath (although you could go straight on over canal and railway, past the church and right on road back to the start)
9. Just before the next bridge divert through car park to walk over the bridges on the road and back to your starting point.

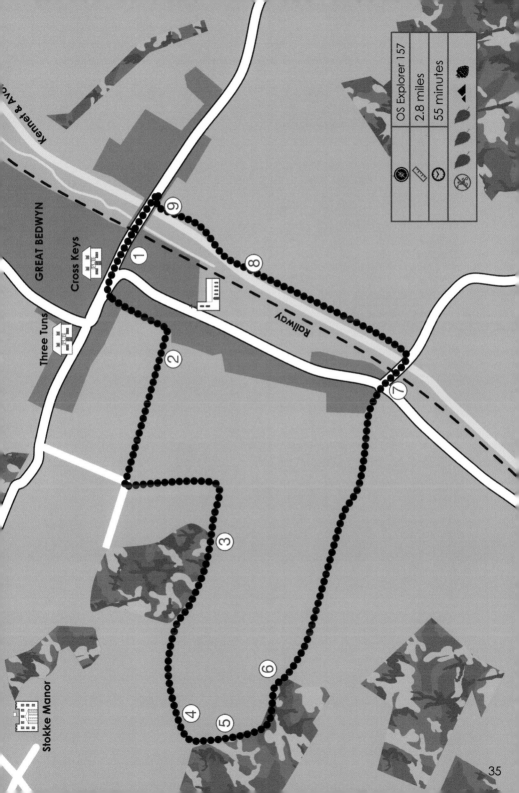

Kennet & Avon

GREAT BEDWYN

Cross Keys

Three Tuns

Stokke Manor

Railway

OS Explorer 157

2.8 miles

55 minutes

1
2
3
4
5
6
7
8
9

8. Great Bedwyn and Chisbury

There are several stiles so not pram friendly, and tricky for dogs. Good for blackberries though.

You've probably noticed that this is the third walk from Great Bedwyn in the book, and I make no apologies for that. Looking at the Ordnance Survey map you will see that the area is littered with footpaths so the problem really was narrowing it down to 3 distinct walks. Each walk has potential for small variations too, especially in the area south east of the village, which could be explored on repeated walks.

Chisbury is a hamlet and prehistoric hill fort. Palaeolithic, Neolithic and Bronze Age artefacts have been found in the area, but the hillfort was most probably built in the late Iron Age in the 1st century AD.

Park either in the **Three Tuns** (if you're going to visit it later) or on **Castle Road**, which is a turning on the road from **Great Bedwyn** to **Little Bedwyn**.

1. Opposite the end of **Castle Road** you will see **a footpath post** with no sign, follow the path between 2 fields. At the end go into the woods following **blue footpath arrow**.

2. Proceed on wide path round to the left, then turn right. When a path branches off to the right continue on main path, but when main path bears left go straight on on smaller path into the trees.

3. Follow muddy path past **Keeper's Cottage** and on to a rickety gate held up with rope on both sides. There are **footpath arrows** on both sides of gate, go through by lifting rope on left side, then go diagonally across field in direction of **yellow arrow**.

4. This path is not obvious, but you are heading two thirds left aiming between a green leafy clump and a large metal gate, and as you get closer you should see a wooden gate stile with a **yellow footpath arrow**.

5. Cross onto lane, then over stile opposite, signposted **Knowle Farm 1½.** Walk along right edge of field to a wooden gate with a gap next to it, go through gap, across path and through another gap and along right edge of next field.

6. At far right corner of field there is a stile with **yellow footpath arrow**, cross stile and turn right, then go through gate and proceed on obvious path along right edge of field.

7. When path emerges onto field turn right and go along right edge of next field. When you reach the end of the field go straight on through a gap in the trees and turn right then bear left to go along right edge of field and at end bear left towards stile.

8. Cross stile and carry on along path between two fences. Cross another stile and carry straight on then left past a large oak tree. Bear right then left (at the end of someone's garden) onto a narrow, nettled, path to emerge next to a telephone box in the centre of **Chisbury**.

9. Head down the road opposite where you emerged, **signposted Great Bedwyn and Chisbury Chapel**, then after about **50 meters** you will see a public footpath sign on your right, marked **Great Bedwyn**, follow this up to and over a stile.

10. Follow **yellow arrow** into field and bear slightly right towards a gap in the fence with a **yellow footpath arrow** on the left hand side. Go through gap and carry straight on until you are heading along right edge of field.

11. Go over stile in bottom right hand corner, following **yellow footpath arrow**, past large muddy patch to continue along right edge of field. After **250 meters** you should see a stile on the right, with **yellow footpath arrow**, cross stile into the woods.

12. Follow fairly clear path past **yellow arrow** on post, the path becomes less clear here, but just continue in same direction and you will join a more obvious path. Follow this path until it spits you out onto the edge of a field.

13. Continue along right edge of field and at end go through gap in trees where you will see a **yellow footpath arrow** pointing straight on and one pointing diagonally left across field.

14. Follow this unclear path heading towards the middle telegraph pole that you can see, then bearing slightly right of it to meet up with the first path of this walk. If you parked on **Castle Road** turn left here back to your car, or otherwise:

15. Head straight on in the same direction, down some little steps and across next field to a gap on left edge. Follow this path down onto a driveway and onto road where you can turn right back to the **Three Tuns**.

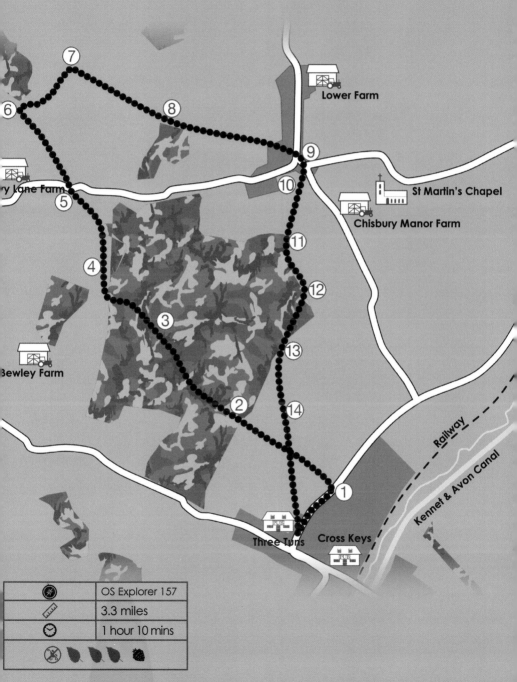

Lower Farm

St Martin's Chapel

Chisbury Manor Farm

ry Lane Farm

Bewley Farm

Three Tuns

Cross Keys

Railway

Kennet & Avon Canal

⊛	OS Explorer 157
📏	3.3 miles
⊙	1 hour 10 mins
⊗ 🍂🍂🍂 🌰	

9. Mildenhall

This is a lovely walk with varied paths. Mildenhall is pronounced Minal. If driving from East on A4 the turn off is signposted **Stitchcombe** and not **Mildenhall.** The shorter version of this walk is obviously easier and stile free, but lacks some nice views.

During the Roman occupation of Britain the fortress town of Cunetio stood in approximately the same site as Mildenhall and the name of the River Kennet, which runs through the town, is thought to be derived from the roman name. The Cunetio Hoard of Roman coins was discovered here in 1978.

In 1881 the Swindon, Marlborough and Andover Railway Company built the Swindon-Marlborough line, the line was closed and the track removed in 1961, but most of the route now serves as the Chiseldon and Marlborough Railway Path, a small section of which is followed in this walk.

Park at or near **The Horseshoe Inn**

1. Go right (west) on road, then after 100 meters turn left down **Church Lane** following a sigh that says '**To the Church**'. Go straight on, past the church, and it's only beyond the end of the road that you can see a **footpath sign** pointing right (west again), follow that along to a kissing gate.

2. After the gate one path bears right and another goes straight on (the **footpath sign** only points right, but I think another has fallen off), follow this one to go along the left edge of the field until after about 500 meters a clear path forks left into the trees.

3. Follow the path round to the right, then left and up some steps to a disused railway line. Turn left along the **Chiseldon and Marlborough Railway Path**, crossing over the **River Kennet**, then over a road (looking left you will see your future route) and to a mileage sign.

4. Go left (**Newbury 22**), then left again down the road and right at T junction, passing **Elcot Orchard** on your right. Pass a pedestrian and cycle path on the right, then take the footpath on the right immediately after that and left along the edge of a field. After about **200 meters** you should see an un-signposted path heading right across field.

5. Follow this path towards the left corner of a new housing estate, then go briefly left then right along edge of estate until you reach a gap in the fence. Cross the lane and go over stile on other side, the up the hill diagonally left, then right until you reach a clear flat path heading left and right.

6. Go left and the path opens into a field, go straight on then start bearing left before a feeding trough. The path isn't very clear but you're heading gradually down hill aiming for the lower edge of the trees, then continuing gradually down aiming for a stile, with footpath sign, back onto the road.

7. Cross stile and turn right on road, then after **10 meters** go left through open gate and follow track that winds down between the bushes. When the path bends to the left there is a metal railing on the right, go past this and double back on the other side of it down smaller path.

8. The path opens out into a track between **the Kennet** and some houses, at the end turn left on the lane and proceed past footpath on the right and modern house on the left, over a bridge until you see a **footpath sign** directing you through a small gap on the left.

9. Take this path then bear slightly right across cricket pitch aiming for a gate at the far right corner. Go through smaller gate next to big one, cross the main road and go left on pavement back to you starting point.

Shorter route

10. Follow **steps 1-4** of longer route.

11. Ignore path on right and continue along left edge of large field until after about half a mile you see a **footpath sign** going left through a gap. Go through and then take the smaller path that starts left of the metal railing.

12. Follow **steps 8-9** of longer route

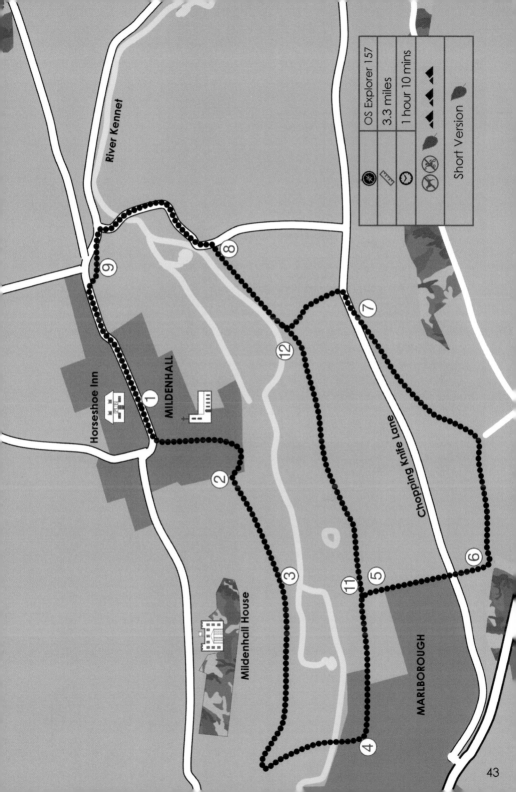

River Kennet

Horseshoe Inn

MILDENHALL

Mildenhall House

Chopping Knife Lane

MARLBOROUGH

	OS Explorer 157
📏	3.3 miles
🕐	1 hour 10 mins
	Short Version

① ② ③ ④ ⑤ ⑥ ⑦ ⑧ ⑨ ⑪ ⑫

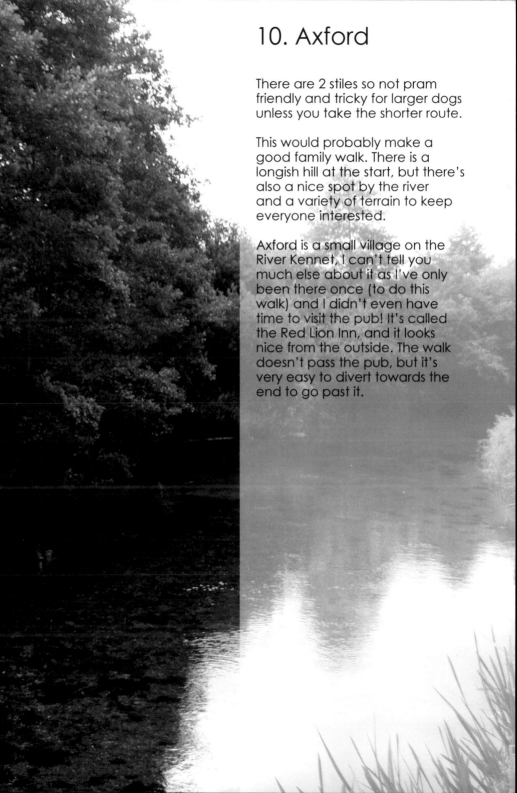

10. Axford

There are 2 stiles so not pram friendly and tricky for larger dogs unless you take the shorter route.

This would probably make a good family walk. There is a longish hill at the start, but there's also a nice spot by the river and a variety of terrain to keep everyone interested.

Axford is a small village on the River Kennet, I can't tell you much else about it as I've only been there once (to do this walk) and I didn't even have time to visit the pub! It's called the Red Lion Inn, and it looks nice from the outside. The walk doesn't pass the pub, but it's very easy to divert towards the end to go past it.

If you drive into Axford from Ramsbury direction you should see the green footpath sign shortly on the left, you can either park on the road near the footpath or carry on to the **Red Lion** and park there and walk back to the footpath.

1. Take the footpath down to a lovely bridge over **The Kennet**, then over a smaller bridge and straight on as the path opens into a track. A **bridleway sign** points right or straight on, go straight on a follow path between trees.

2. Follow wide path gradually up hill, past turning to the left and through a sort of gate, and continue up long slow hill as the path narrows a little, then turns into a grassy path at the end of which a gravel track curls to the right.

3. Go straight on to a stile next to a gate, cross and go along right edge of field, through gate and along right edge of next field until you reach a stile in the corner. Cross this stile, but ignore another one on the left and go down wide path.

4. After **200 meters** there is another stile on left, ignore it and carry on on wide track past farm and through 2 large metal gates. Continue for **400 meters** then go through another large gate then over a stile onto a lane.

5. Turn right on lane (*the path straight on looks enticing, it would leave you with quite a long walk along the main road to finish, but if you're going to the pub you could go this way*) and when the road curls left over bridge go straight on along lane.

6. After about half a mile on the lane you reach a house that you'll recognise from earlier on, turn left and retrace your steps back to the start.

Shorter version.

7. Follow steps 1-2

8. Go right on 2nd gravel path and follow down the hill, past a chalk pit on your right, all the way down to a crossroads, if you've parked at the pub go straight on for the main road and turn right, if not turn right here.

9. Follow step 6

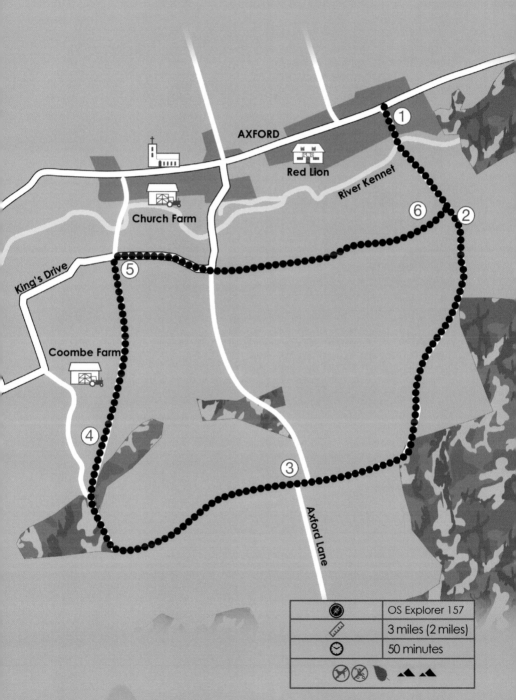

AXFORD

Red Lion

River Kennet

Church Farm

King's Drive

Coombe Farm

Axford Lane

	OS Explorer 157
	3 miles (2 miles)
	50 minutes

11. Ramsbury Manor

3 stiles so not pram friendly although 2 stiles can be avoided in step 2, so probably OK for most dogs. Good for blackberries

This is a pleasant walk which starts by crossing the River Kennet at a lovely bridge, proceeds west to Ramsbury Manor, then loops around countryside to the north and back into Ramsbury.

Ramsbury Manor was built in the 1680s, and was previously home to Sir Francis Burdett (1770 – 1844), a radical Whig politician, and his daughter Angela Burdett-Coutts. In 1837 Angela became the richest woman in England when she inherited her grandfather's fortune. Over several years she gave most of this money away to good causes. By the time she died in 1906, Angela Burdett-Coutts had given away nearly three million pounds. It is now the home of Harry Hyams, the property tycoon who built the office block Centre Point in London.

Park at west end of **Ramsbury High Street** near **Mill Lane** and small post box.

1. Head left down **Mill Lane** and carry straight on as it turns to a gravel track. Go over two bridges and straight on on path until you reach two cottages. Turn right on track along to gate, then proceed on clear path.
2. Follow path for about **500 meters** then when it turns right go straight ahead along little path (you may have to duck under fallen branch) to a stile*. Cross stile and bear slightly left across field on clear path until you reach another stile.
3. Cross into woods then make your way to bridle way to your right and turn right on it heading almost back the way you came. When you reach a junction with road go straight over onto road towards bridge.
4. Go over this bridge and the next one (with nice views of **Ramsbury Manor House** on your left), then at end of drive carefully cross main road and follow public footpath sign pointing left along pavement of road.
5. After about **300 meters** follow bridle way sign to the right on muddy path, past metal gate. After a while you'll climb a steepish bit of hill and eventually reach a small road. Cross over and follow track signposted **Byway to Aldbourne**.
6. Go straight past barn on track, then when the path forks, take the left fork down the hill to a junction of paths. There is a stile that goes into some nettles, go right of this, sort of following a **red byway arrow**, and along left edge of field.
7. Go through open metal gate on the left (or over stile if it's shut) then bear right along right edge of next field to a stile at bottom corner. Cross onto woody path, then along between hedges, then straight on as you pass house on left.
8. As the path bears right you will see a gap in fence ahead of you with a rare **footpath sign** pointing back where you came from, go through and turn right on road. Go straight on past playground on left and straight on on **Hilldrop Close** (but not following the first sign on the right).
9. Follow path after bollards down to road, cross and go through barriers opposite and immediately left down to **Hilldrop Lane** then left on main road and right onto the high street and back to **Mill Lane** where you started.

* to avoid 2 stiles and fallen branch go right then left on gravel path until you reach the junction, where you turn right on road towards bridge. Now follow **step 4**.

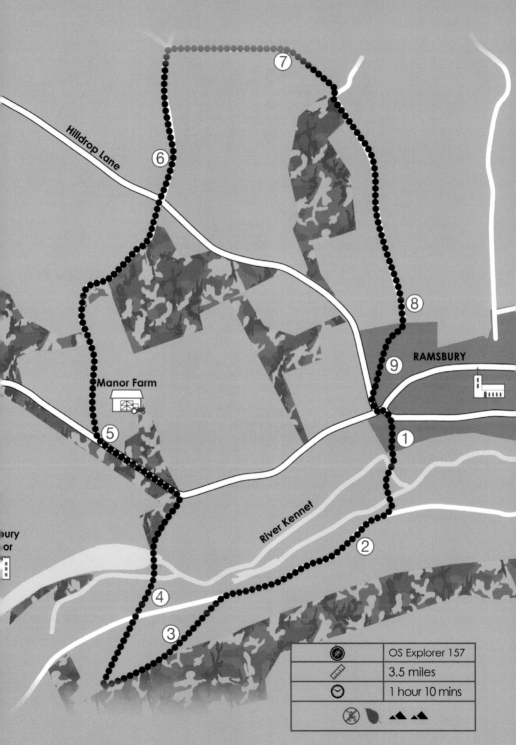

Hilldrop Lane

Manor Farm

RAMSBURY

River Kennet

bury
or

	OS Explorer 157
	3.5 miles
	1 hour 10 mins

12. Ramsbury and South

A few stiles towards the end so not pram friendly, probably OK for most dogs though.

This walk takes you up the hill to the south of Ramsbury where you circumnavigate a ridge that housed a Royal Air Force airfield during the Second World War (not that you can see any evidence of it now) and as you descend, towards the end of the walk you get lovely views of Ramsbury and its church.

Church of England parish church of the Holy Cross dates from the 13th century. In Saxon times, Ramsbury was an important location for the Church, and several of its early bishops went on to become Archbishops of Canterbury. Although no longer a diocesan see, the bishopric of Ramsbury is now an episcopal title used by a suffragan bishop of the Church of England Diocese of Salisbury.

Ramsbury is a busy village with about 2000 residents. It has 2 pubs: The Bell and the Crown and Anchor, both of which serve good food (although The Bell is a little pricey) as well as a primary school, post office and various shops.

Park at, or somewhere near, **The Bell** pub in **Ramsbury**.

1. Walk along the road signposted **Hungerford**, then turn right on road signposted **Froxfield**. Cross bridge then after about **300 meters** you will a **bridle way sign** pointing right and a **footpath sign** pointing left, marked **Littlecote House 2**.
2. Go left on driveway, past **Spring Hill** cottage, then immediately right following **bridleway sign** then slightly left following track along right edge of large field. Continue as it becomes a wide tree-lined path going up the hill.
3. Towards the top of the hill the path forks, keep right. A path joins from the left further along, but carry straight on. The path becomes concrete and as you descend a little goes left or right, but carry straight on along grassy path aiming for far right corner of field.
4. Follow **white footpath arrow** onto muddy path through trees then steeply downhill across a field. At the bottom there are paths heading left, right and straight on, turn right on the proper path, following **yellow footpath arrow**.
5. Carry straight on, ignoring any paths branching off until the path ends at a T-junction with footpath arrows pointing each way, turn right until you reach a small road, turn left on road then at road junction turn right.
6. Walk along road for about **250 meters** then turn right on track towards **Darrell's Farm**. Pass various farm buildings then at the end you will see an obvious path bearing half left between fields.
7. At junction of paths turn right, briefly, then left to carry on in same direction following **yellow footpath arrow**. Bear right on grassy path until you reach a gravely track, turn right on this track and follow to its end.
8. Cross stile with yellow **footpath arrow** on left and head straight down across field to another stile with **footpath signs** pointing right and straight on, cross and go right along path with great views of **Ramsbury** on you left.
9. Continue on path as another path joins, then as it descends gradually you can take either path at the fork and you will end up at a stile at bottom of field, with another broken **yellow footpath arrow**.
10. Cross stile and carry on in same direction across next field towards gap in copse, walk through copse then through a gap stile and onto a track where you turn right and at the end of the track turn left onto the road and back to the start.

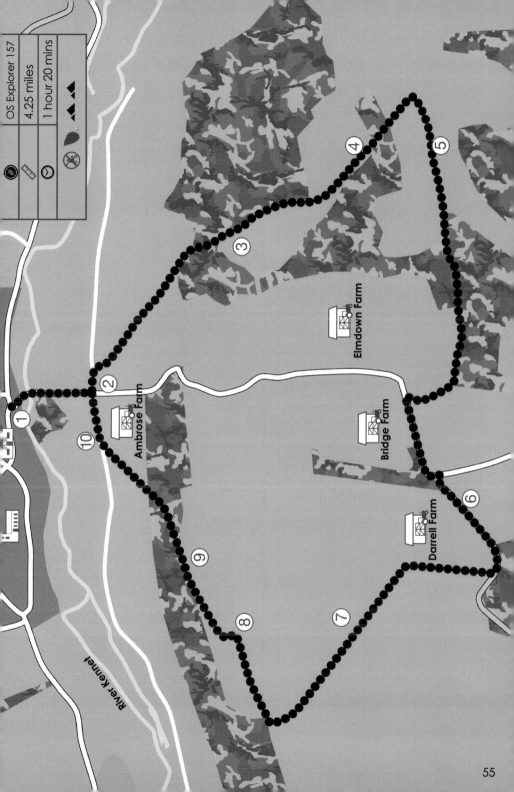

OS Explorer 157

4.25 miles

1 hour 20 mins

Elmdown Farm

Ambrose Farm

Bridge Farm

Darrell Farm

River Kennet

13. Boxford

Dog and Pram friendly (as long as you can get it through 2 large kissing gates).

I have to be honest, this is not the most exciting walk in the world, but it does have the advantage of having easy terrain and no stiles, making it suitable for anyone. Plus the directions are very easy to follow.

It is pleasant at the start walking alongside the River Lambourn and does have two short stretches of path through woodland, the first of which gets a nice carpet of Bluebells when in season, but the second half of the walk follows a wide track and then a road, which is a bit on the dull side.

Boxford is known for the Boxford Masques, an outdoor midsummer celebration held on Hoar Hill in the unspoiled woodland above the village overlooking the Lambourn Valley. It was originally created in the late 19th century by a local writer, Charlotte Peake with her love of music, drama and poetry. The Boxford Masques was performed by locals and lasted only up until the First World War. It was revived in the year 2000 by the Watermill Theatre of Bagnor, near Newbury; it has been very popular since

From the main road take the winding road through **Boxford** bending left then right, then after you've crossed the river you should see a footpath sign on the right, there is a little car park here, but you have to open gate to get to it and it might be open to public, but you can carry on and park near church instead.

1. Walk back to the **footpath sign**, marked **Lambourn Valley Way**, and go through large kissing gate and across to another large kissing gate and onto path between fences.
2. Follow clear path around gate and onto right edge of large field, initially going alongside the **River Lambourn**, and staying on clear path right to the end of this field where a **footpath sign** points you straight on along right edge of next field.
3. At the end you'll see **public footpath signs** pointing right and straight on, go straight on onto path through woods. As soon as you emerge from woods turn left on partially signposted path straight across field.
4. Go through open gateway, past superfluous stile, and straight on following yellow footpath sign through **Bagnor wood** and around to the right. When you emerge from woods turn sharp left following **bridleway sign**.
5. Keep on track as it bears right, then left, down a long straight tree-lined avenue right up to road. Turn left on small road, past **Boxford Farm**, up hill a little bit, then down again, then left at the T junction and back to your starting point.

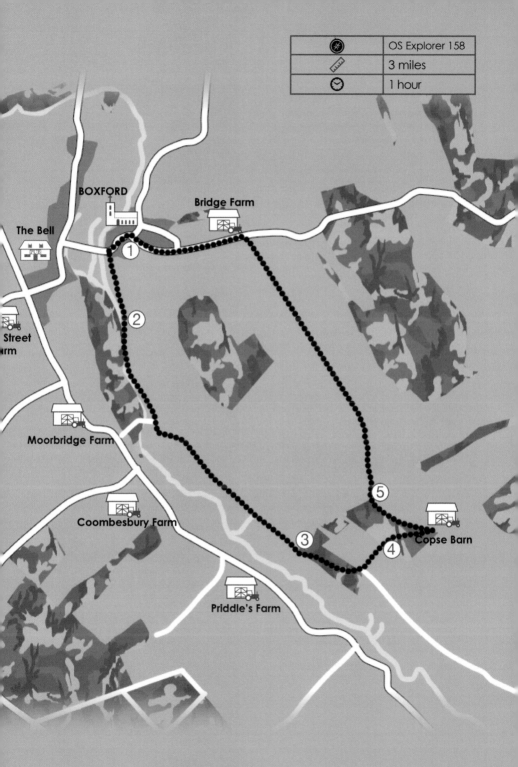

OS Explorer 158

3 miles

1 hour

BOXFORD

Bridge Farm

The Bell

Street
rm

Moorbridge Farm

Coombesbury Farm

Copse Barn

Priddle's Farm

1

2

3

4

5

14. Winterbourne

Winterbourne is a small village situated quite close to the M4 and about 3 miles north west of Newbury. To get there by car you can either head east from Boxford, or follow signs to The Watermill theatre at Bagnor and keep going north from there. It has a nice pub called The Winterbourne Arms which does good food.

The walk is a good, varied walk, which strays briefly into Snelsmore Common, which became a common in the medieval period. It consists of lowland heathland of heather, gorse, wet bog and small trees and broadleaved woodland. There are several rabbit warrens and it is a home to the smaller breeds of deer and other small mammals, snake, lizards and birds such as kestrels and green woodpeckers. Rarer species include the palmate newt and nightjar.

See Walk 15 for more on Snelsmore Common.

Park at, or near, **The Winterbourne Arms** pub.

1. Opposite the pub there is a **footpath signpost** with signs pointing left and right, go right, across grassy patch and over bridge and you will see **two yellow footpaths arrows** pointing straight on and right, go straight on next to fence.

2. When the fence ends bear slightly left and as you cross large field you should soon be able to see a **footpath post** at the far end, aim for this. When you reach post follow **yellow footpath arrow** left briefly along edge of field, then bear right into woods on clear footpath.

3. Follow path with large wire fence on right until you join a larger bridle way going in the same direction. You will see a **yellow footpath arrow** pointing left, but carry straight on on bridleway called **Bebble Lane** and also ignore next turn on left.

4. When you reach a junction of bridle way and footpath turn sharp right on little path into woods on edge of **Snelsmore Common**. When you reach a small road turn right on road for **100 meters** then go over low stile on the right where there are **two footpath signs**, follow the one going furthest left.

5. Follow path down to a kissing gate, then follow **yellow arrow** and **footpath sign** across field to open gate at far side, go through and carry on in same direction, next to row of trees to another kissing gate with **yellow footpath arrow.**

6. Go through and down narrow path to corner of large field. Skirt along right edge of field until you reach a large kissing gate, go through and then right for a few meters on road until you see **footpath sign** pointing left, follow up to field.

7. Walk along left edge of field, then through a gate and along right edge of this field. After superfluous gate bear half left towards a gate with **footpath sign.** Go through and cross road.*

8. To the left of the church is a **public footpath** and **bridleway sign**, follow these down a track, bearing left then right past a disused barn, then when you reach **Lower Farm** bear right.

9. At the end of the fence you should just be able to see a **blue footpath sign** pointing right, follow this along the line of telegraph poles on grassy path between 2 fields, then at junction go straight on along muddy path.

10. Keep going straight on until you pass a house on the right, after which you will see a little gate with a **yellow footpath arrow**, go through and across grass and drive to another gate with an almost hidden **yellow footpath arrow.** Go through gate and walk along gravel driveway back down to your staring point.

*For a shorter version

11. Follow **footpath sign** into church yard. Turn right just before church and you will see a **footpath sign** pointing off to the right, follow this along right edge of large field down and then up the hill.

12. Go through gap at end, following **footpath arrow**, down increasingly narrow path down some steps to the road. Turn left on road back to the **Winterbourne Arms.**

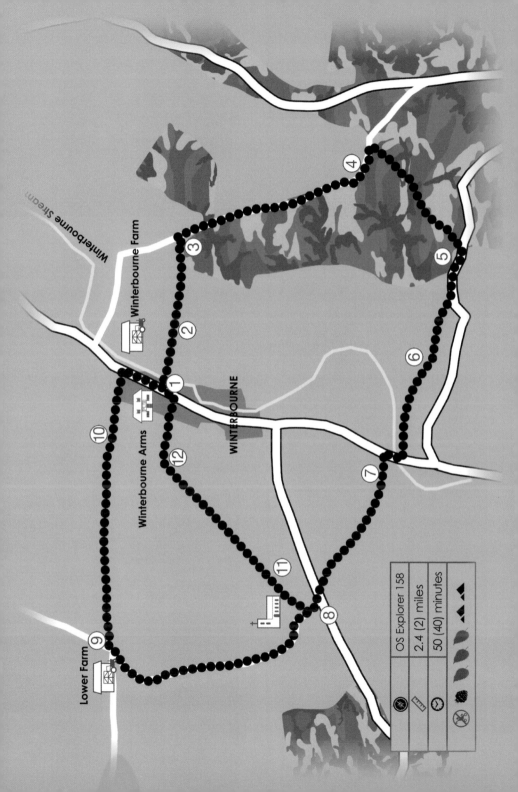

15. Donnington Castle & Snelsmore Common

Dog friendly – pram friendly just about if you take 2nd route avoiding kissing gates.

This is a really nice walk with plenty of variety, although the section between Donnington Castle and Snelsmore Common is a little bit dull. It would be a good walk for kids if you think they can manage 3.4 miles.

Donnington Castle is a ruined medieval castle. It was founded by Sir Richard Abberbury the Elder in 1386 and was bought by Thomas Chaucer, son of poet Geoffrey Chaucer, before the castle was taken under royal control during the Tudor period. During the First English Civil War the castle was held by the royalist Sir John Boys and withstood an 18-month siege; after the garrison surrendered, Parliament voted to demolish Donnington Castle in 1646. Only the gatehouse survives.

During the Second World War Snelsmore Common was taken over by the military, and petrol in jerrycans was stored there for the Normandy landings. Then during 1995-6 the south end of the common became an early base for campaigners protesting against the proposed Newbury bypass. Following eviction of the protesters, the construction of the road went ahead through a part of the common, and an equivalent area of common was added to the west.

Park at **Donnington Castle** car park.

1. At corner of car park there a footpath sign pointing left and towards castle, go up the slope towards the castle. Skirt round right edge of castle along to a gate with footpath sign pointing left.
2. Follow wide track past a couple of houses and a barn and keep going until the track bends to the left, following a **public bridleway** sign. Proceed down to large concrete bridge over the **A34**.
3. Follow path round to the right. After about 300 meters a track branches off to the left, but keep on the main path following a small **footpath sign**. Towards the end of the track there is a footpath heading left (*which you could take for a shorter walk*), carry on on track to skirt left edge of new building.
4. Go through gate into **Snelsmore Common** and follow the path that goes straight on. Shortly you will come to a junction of paths, take the middle path, following a **blue arrow**. Carry on for about 500 meters, passing a bird watching tower on your left, until you come to a **restricted byway** heading left and right, follow the left path.
5. Cross straight over concrete track, following **blue and purple arrows**, then do the same again with another concrete path and you will soon reach another junction of paths, keep following those arrows.
6. As the paths enters some trees there is another junction of paths, follow **the blue arrow** to the left (marked **'BHS Long Distance Route – 3 Downs Link'**). Keep following the **blue arrows** straight on down slightly muddy path until you reach a gate at the edge of **Snelsmore Common**.
7. Go through gate and carry straight on past **Honeyblossom Cottage** and take the left path where the path forks, then straight on where a path heads left (*where short cut would lead to*). Follow tree-lined path, as it becomes narrower and slightly nettley, for about half a mile.
8. Go through a kissing gate on the right, then down a grassy slope and between houses onto the road through **Bagnor** (turn right here for the **Watermill Theatre**). Turn left towards the **Blackbird Pub**, then take the left gravel track after the pub. At the end of the track bear slightly left and go through a kissing gate, following a sign for the **'Lambourne Valley Way'**.
   Alternative step 8 – Ignore gate and continue on path, which becomes narrower and a bit nettley, until you emerge next to a house. Turn left, then left again on concrete path.
9. Follow concrete path up the hill and then over the bridge, then skirt around the 18th tee of the golf course and go left on track, then immediately right following footpath sign into the woods. Go straight on until the path forks, take the right fork to go back to the car park (or left to go back to the castle).

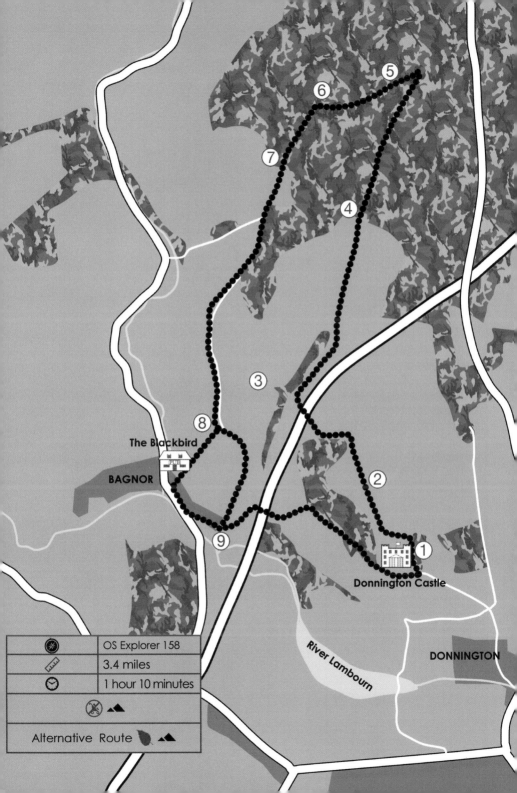

The Blackbird

BAGNOR

Donnington Castle

River Lambourn

DONNINGTON

⊛	OS Explorer 158
📏	3.4 miles
🕐	1 hour 10 minutes
⊗ ▲▲	
Alternative Route 🍃 ▲▲	

16. Stockcross and Bagnor

Dog friendly, tricky with pram as there are narrow bits and a kissing gate.

This a lovely walk which starts in the pleasant village Stockcross, crosses over the River Lambourn, heads along a bit of the Lambourn Valley Way and then along to the edge of Bagnor, where you can either head right and back towards Stockcross or go left past The Watermill Theatre and circle round on a slightly longer route.

The Watermill Theatre was opened in 1967 having been converted from a derelict watermill. It is one of the smallest and most beautiful professional theatres in the country and if you haven't visited it yet you really should. It also has a bar and restaurant should you need sustenance on the walk.

Since doing the walk in 2015 the Lord Lyon pub in Stockcross has apparently closed, but there is another pub, The Rising Sun further up the road and Stockcross is also home to The Vineyard, a rather plush hotel, restaurant and vineyard, which is worth a visit if you can afford it!

I parked at the **Lord Lyon** pub, but you could park anywhere in **Stockcross** really.

1. Turn down **Chapel Lane**, opposite the turning for **Marsh Benham**. Walk past **Stockcross Primary School** and keep straight on, on track, when the road bears right.
2. When the track bears left continue through gate following **yellow footpath arrow** along right edge of field. Go through gate at far corner of field then turn left onto byway. When gravely path bears right keep straight on on smaller path into woods.
3. Follow the wide, but muddy in places, path round to the right, passing **Priddle's Farm** on your right, down to road. Cross and follow **footpath sign** down path into woods.
4. Follow clear path along to a kissing gate, go through, then over wooden bridge onto grassy path next to the **River Lambourn**, with **footpath sign** on fence, then over a stone bridge and proceed past wooden bench to a junction of paths.
5. Follow **the footpath sign** pointing right, into the woods and up a slope until you emerge from woods* there is a footpath sign pointing left here, follow this straight across field towards open gate at far side. **For shorter route go along the Lambourn Valley Way on this pleasant path until it becomes paved and there is a stile on your right, now go to step 9.**
6. Go through gateway and straight on following yellow footpath sign through **Bagnor wood** and around to the right. When you emerge from woods turn right on bridleway.
7. Go diagonally through farmyard until you see a blue footpath arrow pointing left, follow and soon you will see another one pointing right, follow that along long, uneventful, tree-lined bridleway.
8. At a junction of paths head right on bridleway following blue arrow along muddy path then up brief hill and along to a driveway where you can turn left for longer route*, or right, over stile and along drive to another stile for main route.
9. Cross over stile, following **yellow footpath arrow**, along path between 2 fences to cross another stile onto a tree-lined path then over a bridge, along between 2 streams and over another bridge. Go left onto a driveway and follow down to small road.
10. Cross road onto **Snake Lane** and go along lane until after about 500 meters there is a **byway sign** pointing right, follow that. *Or continue on road, then right on main road for a shorter route.*
11. Follow narrow path up hill as it widens into a lovely tree-lined path until you reach a road where you can either go straight on and bear left back to the middle of **Stockcross** or left then right on roads might be quicker for the **Lord Lyon pub**.

*For a longer route:

12. Turn left past houses, and then when you reach a footpath going left follow a **footpath sign** to the right along road. You can bear left over bridge to visit the **Blackbird pub** here, otherwise turn right towards **The Windmill Theatre**.
13. Follow the **byway sign**, next to a bench, left over a narrow concrete bridge, through a gate and along clear path, through another gate, then over another narrow bridge. Go past a superfluous kissing gate and bear right on clear path until you reach a junction of byway and bridleway next to a large gate.
14. Continue on byway on the **'BHS long distance route, three downs link'** apparently. Follow path down to road and turn right. After about **200 meters** you will see a **public footpath sign** pointing right, turn left on **Snake Lane** and follow from **step 10** above.

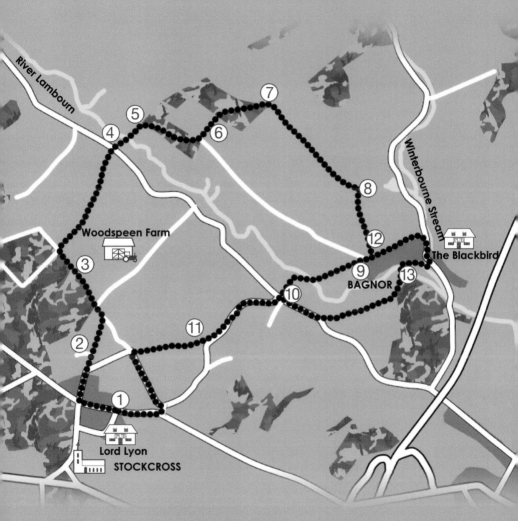

⊛	OS Explorer 158
📏	3.3 / 3.8 / 3.1 miles
🕐	1:10 / 1:20 / 1:00

17. Hamstead Marshall

Dog friendly, pram friendly only if you can get through 3 kissing gates and a narrow bit of path.

Hamstead Marshall is a small village with a lot of history. In the 12th and 13th Centuries it was home to the Earl Marshal, the monarch's chief adviser and administrator. The manor continued to be owned and used by kings and queens throughout the centuries, until it was sold in 1613.

The village was from 1620 until the 1980s the seat of the Earls of Craven. William Craven, 1st Earl of Craven (1608-1697) built a mansion there, originally intended as a residence for Charles I's sister, Elizabeth of Bohemia, although she died before construction began. It burnt down in 1718. The Grade 1 listed gate piers that you will see in step 2 of the walk are all that's left of the original mansion.

The Cravens later expanded a hunting lodge to live in instead, and this still stands, privately occupied, in the centre of Hamstead Park. The family still owned the property up to the 1980s when it was put up for auction.

This is a lovely walk that starts at the White Hart pub in the village and heads along, past Craven House, into the picturesque Hampstead Park and back to the village. The last ½ mile is all road, but this is unavoidable unfortunately.

Park at the **White Hart** pub in **Hampstead Marshall**.

1. Go right on the road, past the front of the pub and shortly you will see a **public bridleway sign** pointing right, follow this past farm buildings then along clear wide path between fences until you reach a gate next to a wooden bench.
2. Go through gate and cross road, then follow **footpath sign** through kissing gate and onto clear path between ferns. Go through another kissing gate at top of small hill then head across field in direction of distant gateposts (known as **gate piers** apparently).
3. Keep heading towards the gateposts even when a track bears right and you should find the path that skirts left of the first gateposts, with **Craven House** to your left. Follow path towards gate and go through large kissing gate, past more gateposts and turn right on footpath.
4. Follow gravelly path round to the left, then when it forks bear right and then right again to join concrete path. There are some nice views of the **River Kennet** to the left and there is a smaller path you can follow, for a while, for a closer view.
5. Keep on concrete path as it winds past the lake, up the hill and round to the left. Ignore turning to the left, but shortly afterwards leave the main path as head down towards a kissing gate next to a metal gate and go through either.
6. Proceed straight on across field to rejoin the concrete path next to **footpath signs**. Go left on path and before it bears left there are more **footpath signs** and you will see a wooden gate to your right with a **yellow footpath arrow**.
7. Go through and head in a straight line across field until it dips down to a gate leading onto a narrow path. Keep on this clear path, with fence on your left, following an occasional **yellow footpath arrow** until you eventually reach a gate.
8. Go through gate and right onto road and stay on it, ignoring turning to the right, for nearly half a mile until you reach the **White Hart** pub.

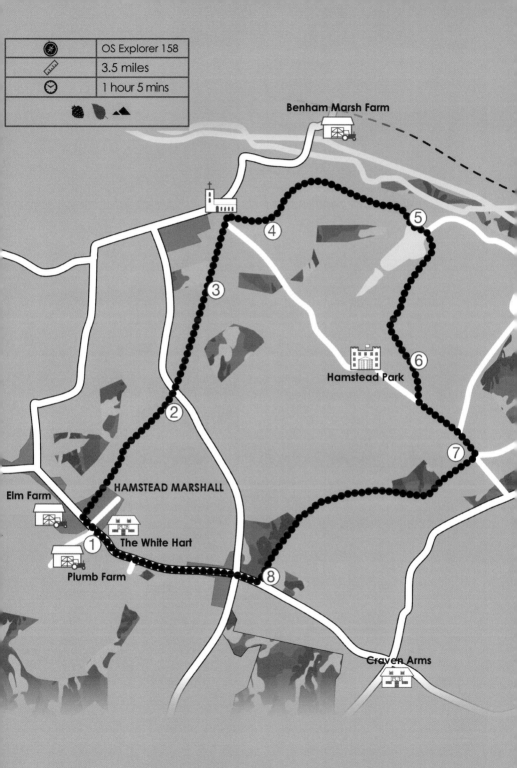

OS Explorer 158

3.5 miles

1 hour 5 mins

Benham Marsh Farm

⑤

④

③

⑥

Hamstead Park

②

⑦

HAMSTEAD MARSHALL

Elm Farm

①

The White Hart

Plumb Farm

⑧

Craven Arms

18. Kintbury and Inkpen

Kintbury is a very pleasant village situated next to the Kennet and Avon canal and the railway line heading to Paddington. It has a connection to Jane Austen, whose family were close friends with the Fowle family of Kintbury and it is believed that Jane would have visited and stayed at the Vicarage (now home to novelists Robert Harris and Gill Hornby) many times.

This walk starts at Saint Mary's Church in the centre of Kinbury and heads south to skirt along the edge of the sprawling village of Inkpen, before passing St Cassians Centre, a Catholic youth retreat centre, on the way back to Kinbury.

As well as the Church, there are 3 pubs in Kintbury; The Dundas Arms, The Blue Ball and the Prince of Wales, plus a primary school, a corner shop, a butcher's and a lovely café and cake shop called Cocochoux.

Park near the **Saint Mary's Church** in **Kintbury**, or at the **Blue Ball pub** if you're going to go there (but car park is quite small)

1. Follow **public footpath sign** into churchyard and fork left on path, then turn left again on tree-lined path and out through gate onto gravel path opposite. Follow path between houses and left round the **Blue Ball pub** down to road.

2. Cross road and follow **public footpath sign** on little road then on path between 2 fences, which turns into lovely tree-lined path. Go through gate at end of path, along short path and through another gate, then bear left on path.

3. Go through gate at end of path then along left edge of field. Cross stile and proceed along right edge of next field to a low and narrow stile at the far end, go through and turn left on road.

4. Ignore footpath signs pointing left after 10 and 250 meters, then when road bears left there is a footpath sign pointing right and a gate straight ahead. Go through gate and along path to another low stile.

5. Cross stile and continue along right edge of field, then across another stile and down to road. Cross road and go through gate on other side to a path along right edge of field. Follow **footpath sign** left then continue round to the right towards gate.

6. Go through gate and bear right along path next to wooden fence, then when you emerge onto larger path bear right/straight on following **public bridleway sign** and around to the road. Cross road then bear half left on 2nd road, signposted **Swan Inn** and follow this road on the outskirts of **Inkpen.**

7. Ignore unmarked path on right after about **250 meters**, until after another **250 meters** a broken **byway sign** points you down a clear track into the woods (**The Folly**). After **400 meters** a byway branches back and left, ignore this and carry on on path as it turns into a public bridleway with concrete base, then gravel, then concrete again until you eventually see a 5 way **footpath junction sign** in the hedge to the right.

8. Follow the **yellow arrow**, first right, down what looks like someone's drive. Go through large gate and bear right then left on road, then after about 100 meters there's a small gap in the hedge on your left with a **yellow footpath arrow** leading you over a little bridge and to a gate.

9. Go through gate and head right on clear path across field. Go through gate at end of field and across bridge onto path straight on through woods (**High Trees**). Go through gate and onto field.

10. Bear slightly right towards a waymark post on field, then continue straight on, with **St Cassian's College** on your right, towards a 4 way **footpath junction sign** and straight on past that to go through gate at end of field, and through copse.

11. Continue on clear path across field, skirting past right edge of woods, towards a gate and **footpath sign**. Go through gate, cross road and through large kissing gate on other side and straight on across field to another large kissing gate.

12. Go left on wide footpath, passing a house on your left, around a large gate and straight on on **Wallington's Road** and back up to main road through **Kintbury** and the **Blue Ball pub**. Retrace your steps back to the start.

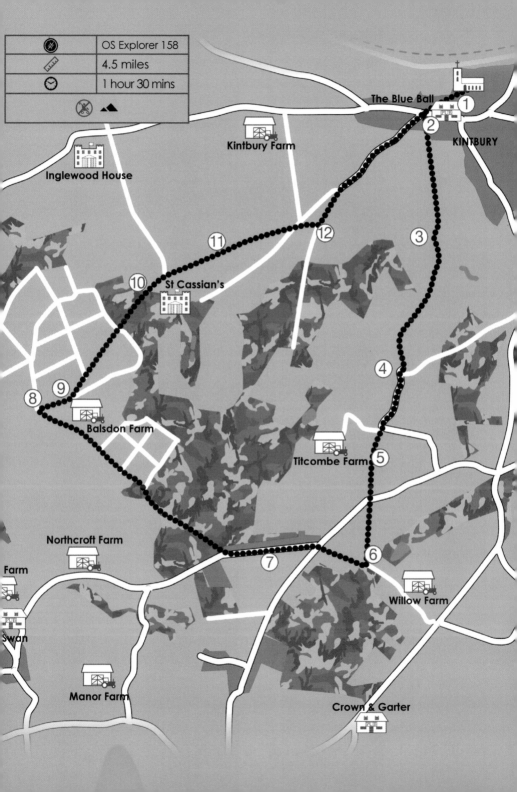

19. Inkpen Circuit

Inkpen is a strange sort of village in that its properties, school, village hall and two pubs (The Swan and the Crown & Garter) are widely spread out across quite a large area, connected by a network of small twisting roads that it is very easy to get lost on when driving.

There are plenty of different circuits you could walk around Inkpen, but there aren't many convenient places to park so this one starts at The Swan pub and does an easy circuit from there.

In step 5 if you were to turn right rather than left at junction you would come across a large field of Mediterranean crocuses, one of only two in the UK. It is Britain's largest display of this non-native plant and attracts botanists from across the country. From early March for about a month, the eight-acre field is a splendid sight, with purple and white crocus heads - some plain, others striped - dotting the grassland.

Inkpen parish documents have recorded the displays for at least 200 years. Nobody is sure how the crocuses arrived in the field, but one legend is that 12th-century Crusaders brought them back from Europe as a source of saffron to flavour food, although it may be more likely they were for herbal and medicinal purposes.

Park at **The Swan** pub in **Inkpen**, there aren't really any other parking options so you'll have to have something at the pub, or buy something from their farm shop.

1. Turn left out of pub car park, on path along front of pub, then along road past the left turn, then right at junction, and after about **10 meters** you should see a partially concealed **public footpath sign** pointing left.
2. Follow sign onto gravel path, then smaller path bearing left then right along the backs of houses and fields and along several wooden platforms and over a wooden bridge to a gate.
3. Go through or around gate and follow grassy path around to the right, then dog-leg left path past a house and at end of path cross small road and follow **footpath sign** through kissing gate and straight across field to another kissing gate.
4. Go through and ignoring tempting paths to left and right go straight on through another gate, along a short path, up 2 steps and through a gate onto a track. Turn left on track and bear left as it turns into a smaller path.
5. When you come to a footpath junction turn left, then shortly right along drive with house/mansion behind you until you emerge next to **Inkpen Primary School**. Turn left on road, past junction going left, then shortly after that turn right on track signposted **Haycroft Cottages**.
6. Follow winding track past various houses until you reach a junction with **byway signs** pointing left and right. Go left and carry on on path as it turns into a public bridleway with concrete base, then gravel, then concrete again until you eventually see a 5 way **footpath junction sign** in the hedge to the right.
7. Take the first left path, almost going back on yourself between 2 tall hedges. Follow yellow arrow slightly to the left and down narrow path to footbridge, then turn right up to large kissing gate.
8. Go through gate and follow **yellow footpath arrow** along right edge of field, over a stepped stile next to gate, and all the way along the right edge of the next field until eventually you come to another stile.
9. Cross stile and go right on lane down to large gate which you can go through or over stile next to it. Turn right at main road and after about 20 meters there is a **footpath sign** pointing right. Cross stile and go along right edge of field.
10. Turn right towards stile and cross onto concrete bridge over stream, then follow path around and across another bridge and up to a gate. Go through or around gate, then left on path between 2 fences, which turns into a track that leads to main road where you turn left and back to **The Swan pub**.

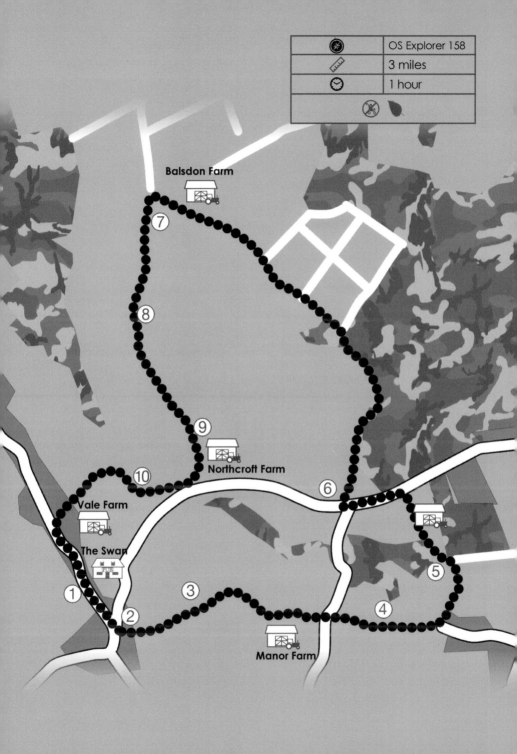

20. East Woodhay

For this walk I appear to have inadvertently strayed into Hampshire, but it's worth going that little bit further for a pleasant walk that was for me at least all completely unknown territory.

The parish of East Woodhay contains a number of villages and hamlets, including Ball Hill, Heath End, Hatt Common, Woolton Hill and East End. The last two contain schools: Woolton Hill Junior School, St Thomas's Church of England Infant School, and St. Martin's Church of England Primary School. The parish also has a small, triangular village green containing a war memorial and was once the site of the village stocks.

Park next to **East Woodhay Church**. **East Woodhay** is not that easy to find. I followed signs for **West Woodhay** from **Kintbury**, then signs for **East Woodhay**, but at the penultimate junction there are no signs at all (turn right) and at the last one turn left signposted **East end**.

1. Walk down the road with large stone wall on your right, then cross stile, into field. Go diagonally across in direction of **footpath sign** on fairly clear path to another stile, cross keep going in same direction across next field to a stile next to a large metal gate.

2. Cross stile and road and head down track opposite, following **footpath sign**. At end of track bear slightly left next to metal gate over a low stile and follow path between two fences. Cross stile at end and go left following **yellow footpath arrow**.

3. Follow grassy track past a large barn, then just before the next barn you should see a **yellow footpath arrow** (and a sign saying **'Hayes'**) pointing right, follow this through farmyard and onto a small road.

4. Follow road around to the right (ignoring footpath to the left) then left. And at T junction turn right. Go past left turn then turn left at T junction then shortly right on unmarked track, then through gate or over stile onto path between hedge and fence.

5. Go through kissing gate onto another path between paddocks, through another kissing gate and follow direction of yellow footpath arrow to skirt left edge of pond (in the gardens of **Northenby**) and over bridge at far corner of field.

6. Turn right on footpath up a small slope and go through gate or over stile, but leave main path and bear half left across field in direction of stile towards another stile. Cross this stile and shortly another one, then go straight on when the path forks.

7. Cross stile at end of path and go left briefly on road, then follow **bridleway sign** to the right onto muddy, then grassy, then gravely path. Turn right after house, past some old farm buildings and onto a track at the end of which is a stile with a **yellow footpath arrow**.

8. Cross stile and follow path round into large field, then when the path forks bear slightly right across field to a stile, cross and continue in same direction across next field to another stile at the far right corner. Cross and follow path past houses and onto road.

9. Turn left on road and then take road signposted **East Woodhay**, then after **200 meters** there is partly concealed **footpath sign** pointing right, leading down to a stile with two **yellow footpath arrows**, cross and bear left across field.

10. As you go through gap in hedge, next to post, the path forks, take the right fork and proceed to a small stile just left of a metal gate. Cross stile and head left following **yellow footpath arrow** to another stile at far corner. Cross onto path through wood and along to black gate. Go through, then left on gravel path back to the church.

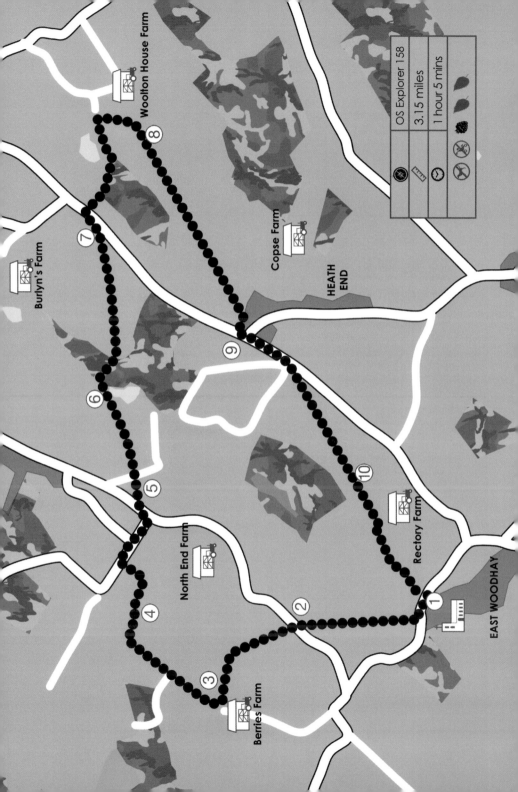

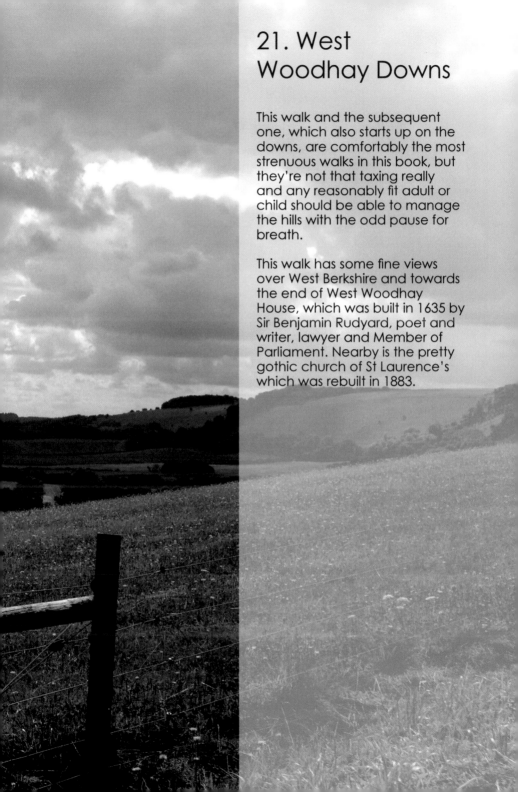

21. West Woodhay Downs

This walk and the subsequent one, which also starts up on the downs, are comfortably the most strenuous walks in this book, but they're not that taxing really and any reasonably fit adult or child should be able to manage the hills with the odd pause for breath.

This walk has some fine views over West Berkshire and towards the end of West Woodhay House, which was built in 1635 by Sir Benjamin Rudyard, poet and writer, lawyer and Member of Parliament. Nearby is the pretty gothic church of St Laurence's which was rebuilt in 1883.

Drive up towards **Combe Gibbet** (signposted from **Inkpen**) then turn left at car park, down the hill then sharp right back up again to unmarked car park at top.

1. Go right on track that runs behind car park then after **200 meters** there are footpaths leading left and right, go right through bushes and over (at time of writing) broken stile, then follow fairly clear path half left across field.

2. Head down and past a completely superfluous stile with **yellow arrow** pointing the way, and keep on path along ridge heading gradually downhill until you cross a stile to a path going into the woods.

3. Follow winding path through woods to emerge onto small road, cross and follow **footpath sign** opposite, winding down narrow path and the left along left edge of large field until you come next to the road.

4. Do not go onto road, but follow **2ⁿᵈ footpath sign** back along left edge of same field. About half way along edge you'll see a **yellow footpath arrow** pointing left, follow that along track and stay on track as it bends left then right.

5. When you come to some farm buildings with paths going different ways, you want to take the bridleway going sharp right. After **100 meters** a track forks left, but carry straight on for another **200 meters** and this time bear left with the track up hill to a gate.

6. Go round the side of the gate, cross small road, and past another gate, following **wooden footpath sign** onto chalk path up the hill. After about **500 meters** a path quite clearly bears left across field, follow this path all the way across the field. (Or carry straight on if you want to cut out a corner).

7. At the end turn right on grassy bridle way. Go over or around strange looking gate, then carry on on clear and slightly muddy path for another **500 meters** then go around a large log on path and left onto road.

8. Cross road and follow **footpath sign** over stile on the right. Bear half right on unclear path aiming for right edge of woods, the path becomes clearer here and criss-crosses another path. Great views here of **West Woodhay House** and most of the walk you've just done.

9. Bear left on other path going past **footpath sign** on corner post of woods then diagonally up across field to gate in corner. (you could avoid the last hill by staying parallel to road along top). Go through gate and cross road back to car park.

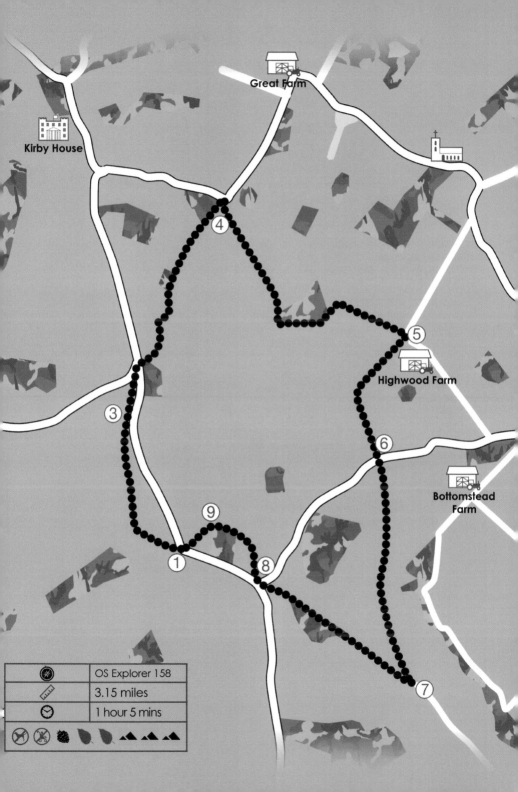

Great Farm

Kirby House

Highwood Farm

Bottomstead
Farm

④

③

⑨

①

⑧

⑤

⑥

⑦

OS Explorer 158

3.15 miles

1 hour 5 mins

22. Combe Gibbet and Village

This walk starts on Walbury Hill which, at 297 meters, is the highest point in South East England. It is the starting point of the Test Way, which heads down to Southampton, and the Wayfarers Walk, which goes all the way down to Emsworth, near Portsmouth. This walk heads down the hill to the south and through the pretty village of Combe, then back up a steep hill onto the downs and past the Combe Gibbet.

The Gibbet you pass is a replica of the original, which was erected in 1676 for the sole purpose of gibbeting the bodies of George Broomham and Dorothy Newman, who had murdered George's wife and son after they had discovered the two of them together on the downs. The gibbet was only ever used for them and was placed in such a prominent place as a deterrent for others.

This part of the downs is now a popular spot for hang gliders and paragliders and on any pleasant and breezy weekend day you will find them launching themselves from the northern slopes.

If you follow signs for **Combe Gibbet** from **Inkpen** there is a car park at the top of the hill on the left, park here.

1. Start left on footpath **(Wayfarer's Walk)** and you will shortly reach a fork in the path, take either as they both go the same way. Carry on for almost 1km (across **Walbury Hill**) until you see footpaths to the left and right. (spot the cover of my first book).

2. Cross the stile on the right and head down and left across field on fairly clear path until a clearer path crosses, head downhill on this path towards gate. On left gate post a **yellow arrow** points you down into a copse, follow this narrow path.

3. Soon you come to a marked bridle way, keep right on this path, then again at next path junction, then through gate at bottom of hill where a bridle way goes left and straight on, go straight on past a farm house as the path turns into a road.

4. Follow road down into **Combe**, ignoring a footpath on the left, past **Jon Snow**'s house (you'll have to guess which one it is) and right at the T junction, signposted '**Hungerford 6**'. After 500 meters take a left turn on the road marked **Wright's Farm**, then follow round to the right.

5. As the roads bends right again a **Public Bridleway** sign points straight on, follow this past farm and when the path forks go left and you'll see a **public bridleway** sign next to gate and high stile. Cross stile and head straight across and up the field aiming for the far right corner where there is another gate and stile (you may need a rest here).

6. Cross stile and the path forks slightly left where the track bends right, follow the path (although you could cut the corner on the track, but it's not a public right of way), through the fields, then take a right on the bridle way (on the **Test Way**) until you reach the main path and turn right again.

7. This track goes towards and around the **Combe Gibbet** then down to the car park where you started. There are gates before and after Gibbet to take a closer look, the first gate suggests that it's only for use of **Thames Valley Hang Gliding Club**, but I wouldn't worry about that, especially as the far gate is less prohibitive.

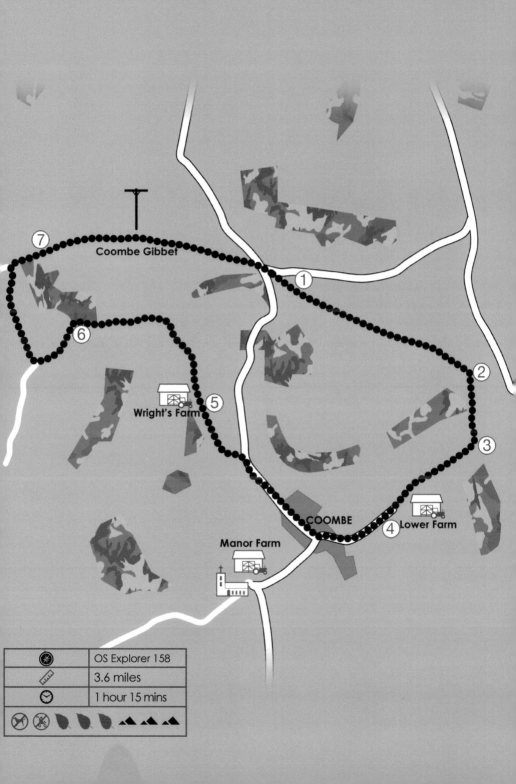

Coombe Gibbet

⑦

⑥

①

②

③

⑤

Wright's Farm

④ Lower Farm

COOMBE

Manor Farm

◉	OS Explorer 158
📏	3.6 miles
🕐	1 hour 15 mins

23. Upper Chute

No stiles so dog friendly, possible with a good buggy, but some bits of path are quite muddy so quite difficult.

I looked a bit further afield for these last two walks in an effort to find more buggy friendly walks and I pretty much succeeded in that neither has any stiles, but some of the woodland paths are quite narrow and/or muddy so they're not going to be easy with a buggy/pram.

The paths in Collingbourne Wood bear little relation to what you see on the OS map, and to be honest the walk that follows was not what I intended to do when I set out because of this, but if you follow the instructions carefully you should end up following the same route as I did. It's not just in the woods either, according to the OS map there should be a path leading from near the end of step 7 back to the starting point, but I certainly couldn't find it, and if you look carefully at the start/end you can see a public footpath sign pointing into a field with no means for you to get into the field!

Park at or near the **Cross Keys** pub in **Upper Chute**. Driving from Hungerford direction; go south towards **Salisbury**, and after passing Shalbourne take a left signposted **Oxenwood**, go right at **Oxenwood** then follow signs for **Chute**, then **Upper Chute**, then **The Cross Keys**.

1. Head down unmarked track opposite the **Cross Keys** pub, past a couple of house on the right, then bear right with path as you pass some farm equipment. Bear left with path and head down towards **Collingbourne Woods**.

2. As you enter woods bear slightly left past house, then shortly afterwards follow a **public bridleway sign** pointing to the right. Carry straight on on occasionally muddy path until an obvious path crosses perpendicular to yours, turn right here.

3. After about **150 meters** the path forks, take the left fork. Follow path round to the left. Ignore 2 right turns, but do turn right when you reach a T junction. Keep left when the path forks.

4. Cross over a sunken path that crosses left to sharp right, but at next sunken path turn right. The path rises to a normal level then winds its way through the trees for about **400 meters** until it joins with a larger, straight path, turn right on this path.

5. Ignore path that crosses. Follow path that is rutted with tyre marks and quite muddy, but go straight on when the larger track bears left. Keep on path as it bears left then right around the end of a field, then after **100 meters** as on path veers to the left look right and you will see a large metal gate.

6. Go through gate and head straight across field, aiming for the right edge of copse, then as you reach it you will join a clearer path heading down hill along the left edge of field.

7. At bottom left corner of field go left through open gate, then right onto path continuing in same direction as before up a fairly steep hill ignoring 2 turns to the left, but at top of hill bear left with track, then right, ignoring track that goes sharp left.

8. Go straight on at junction of **byways** and up another steep hill until the path turns into a road and comes out at the **Cross Keys** pub.

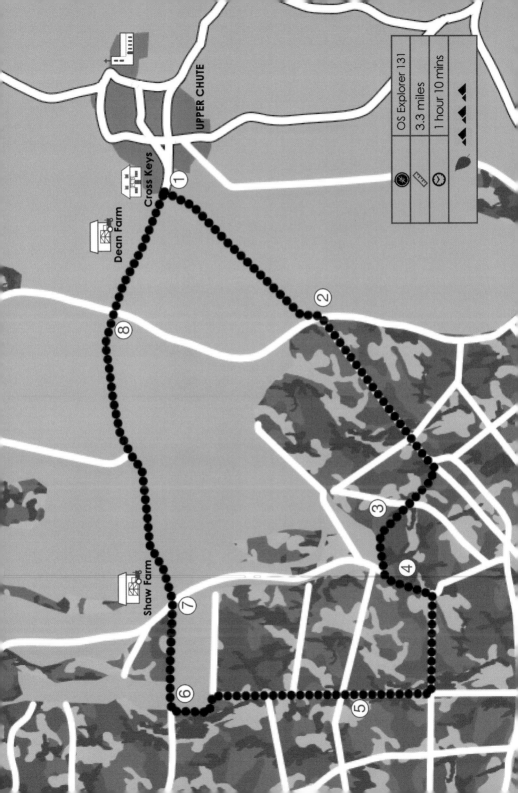

UPPER CHUTE

Cross Keys

Dean Farm

Shaw Farm

①
②
③
④
⑤
⑥
⑦
⑧

✳	OS Explorer 131
📏	3.3 miles
⏱	1 hour 10 mins
🍃	▲▲ ▲▲ ▲▲ ▲▲

24. Collingbourne Woods from the west

No stiles so dog friendly, possible with a good buggy, but some bits of path are quite muddy so quite difficult.

This last walk had a slightly odd gestation. Like the previous walk it was devised in an attempt to find more buggy friendly walks (which it to some extent is), but I only picked the starting point because I knew of The Shears pub, which is a very nice, somewhat out of the way pub, with good food, and I only knew of The Shears because it's on a handy short cut if you're driving from Hungerford to Salisbury.

The walk is quite a nice mix of terrains with no stiles, but potentially some quite muddy bits. There is room for a certain amount of variation once you reach the woods, but just be careful because as I mentioned in the previous walk, the paths through the woods don't bear much relation to what's on the OS map.

Park at or near **The Shears** pub near **Collingbourne Ducis**. Driving from **Hungerford** direction; go south towards **Salisbury**, then turn left at a sign for **Wexcombe** and follow this long, mostly straight road and when you see a turning for **Collingbourne Ducis** on the right turn left for The Shears pub.

1. Head left on road (if coming out of pub car park), which soon turns into a track. After about **250 meters** you will see a **byway sign** and a **bridleway sign**, both pointing in roughly the same direction, but after **100 meters** the bridleway does fork off to the right, follow this path.

2. Proceed on this wide path, up a long gentle hill, for about **500 meters**, then go straight on when a path crosses left and right. At the top of the hill as the path gets a bit bumpy and muddy look out for an unmarked gate on the left and go through gap next to it.

3. Head towards a large open blue gate and go through, then proceed across field. There is no obvious path across, but just head towards far corner where you should see another open blue gate, go through this and bear right.

4. After just **10 meters** or so you will see a small gap in woods on your right, go through gap and go left along small path in woods. When the path leads to edge of woods again take the path that turns right into the woods.

5. Follow narrow and muddy path straight, ignoring any paths branching on either side, until you come to a much larger path going left to right with a public bridleway sign ahead. Go left on very straight bridleway up very gentle hill.

6. When the path eventually bears a little right you will see a footpath that forks off to the left, follow this and keep left as a couple of tributaries branch right. Towards the end of the path there is a junction of paths, turn right.

7. Follow this muddy and well hooved path down to a gravely track where you will turn left. Ignore turning on right and after about **300 meters** or so there is an obvious turning on the left, follow this path.

8. Keep following this long wide byway until you reach a large blue gate. Go round the gate and straight on on byway and after **100 meters** you will see the bridleway you took at the start of the walk, carry straight on back to your starting point.

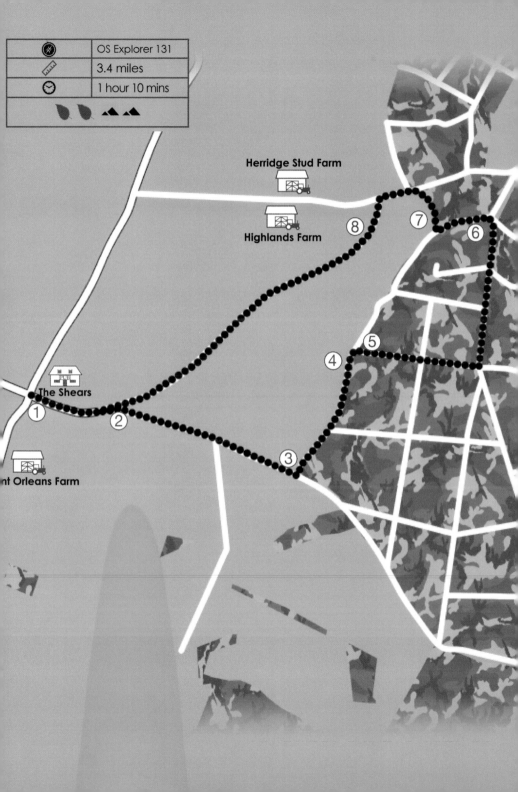

the HARROW at little bedwyn

A Michelin Star Restaurant
and rated as one of the UK's top 50 restaurants.

Tel: 01672 870871

Email: office@theharrowatlittlebedwyn.com

Booking Essential

 @littlebedwyn

The Harrow at Little Bedwyn, Marlborough, Wiltshire SN8 3JP
Tel: 01672 870871. Email: office@theharrowatlittlebedwyn.com
www.theharrowatlittlebedwyn.com
www.rogerjonesconsultancy.com

1 High St, Great Bedwyn, Wiltshire SN8 3NU
Tel: 01672 870280
eat@tunsfreehouse.com | www.tunsfreehouse.com

hungerford
BOOKSHOP

We sell a wide range of books from timeless classics to exciting new reads. Thousands of good quality second-h books are available downstairs too!

Pop in for a browse or for some recommendations. We also sell cards, stationery and book tokens.

Not got what you're looking for?

Then take advantage of our fast ordering service.

Ask about forthcoming author events

24 High Street, Hungerford, Berkshire RG17 0NF

01488 683480 www.hungerfordbooks.co.uk